THE BLACK MADONNA

FRED GUSTAFSON

Best wishes !

Fred Gustafson

December 1994

The Black Madonna of Einsiedeln.

THE BLACK MADONNA

FRED GUSTAFSON

SIGO PRESS

BOSTON

● SIGO PRESS
25 New Chardon Street, #8748
Boston, Massachusetts 02114

Publisher and General Editor, Sisa Sternback

Library of Congress Cataloging-in-Publication Data

Gustafson, Fred
    The Black Madonna / Fred Gustafson.
        p.   cm.
    Includes bibliographical references and index.
    ISBN 0-938434-49-7, — ISBN 0-938434-48-9 (pbk.)
    1. Black Virgins, 2. Goddesses. 3. Femininity of God. 4. Lilith
(Semitic mythology) 5. Women and religion. I. Title.
BT670.B55G83   1990
291.2'114—dc20   90-39884
                                                           CIP

Printed in Korea

Table of Contents

Illustrations

Following page 78

Introduction

A number of years ago I visited the Benedictine Monastery in Einsiedeln, Switzerland, where I first saw the statue of the Virgin Mother popularly known as the Black Madonna of Einsiedeln. Only later did I find out that she was one of scores of such black-hued madonnas throughout Europe. Looking back, I recall just how unconscious I was of her significance at first, though I did know something profound was touched within me. This something only later became clear.

The Black Virgin of Einsiedeln is not an isolated entity, but the product of many collective psychological forces that have influenced European history for hundreds of years. In his recent book, *The Cult of the Black Virgin*, Ean Begg provides a thorough and succinct analysis of these many forces, both real and speculative, which have produced and sustained the Black Madonna phenomenon. Begg also presents a gazetteer of the some four hundred Black Madonnas throughout the world, and at the same time questions why, being so spiritually powerful, they seem so little known.

Today the archetype of the feminine is coming to the fore world-wide, and with it a renewed interest in the Black Virgins. At Einsiedeln alone, hundreds of thousands of pilgrims visit the shrine of the Black Madonna every year. Her specific historical roots go back a thousand years and are deeply embedded in Swiss history. Yet pilgrims from all over the world are touched by her, by an aspect of the feminine embodied by her yet not normally acknowledged. This darker aspect of the feminine has throughout history been both feared and sought after, both hated and admired. The Black Madonna of Einsiedeln stands among the many Black Virgins that seem to imagistically express this dark side of the feminine in a creative transformational manner for both the individual and the collective.

The larger repercussions of the Black Madonna phenomenon became clearer as I read Heinrich Zimmer's book, *Art and Symbol in Indian Myth and Civilization,* in which he provides a very sensitive description of the Indian goddess Kali, who is greatly loved, terribly horrific and entirely black. I immediately made the connection with the Black Madonna at Einsiedeln—a connection that unlocked a host of questions regarding the dark side of the feminine within myself and within the culture around me.

It is not my purpose to discuss at any length the process of my own individuation as far as integrating the feminine principle is concerned, let alone its dark side. It is enough to say that I am male, white and of a Protestant background to suggest to most readers why the dark goddess would have some appeal to me. At the same time, the profoundly personal dimension of this study found parallels in the lives of people with whom I worked as an analyst and pastoral counselor, both men and women from a wide range of backgrounds.

It is not easy to quickly or simply answer the question of what the Black Madonna actually represents. One answer leads to more questions which in turn demand more explanations. A possible reason for this turmoil lies in the difficulty our culture has always had in consciously integrating the feminine side of life, and especially its dark side. Another reason is the nature of the dark feminine itself, which defies attempts to give eternally fixed limits to what she represents.* Still, she reflects herself in our personal and collective lives and gives intimations of her most essential meaning through images, myths, dreams, and fantasies. If we are willing to receive and be open to such phenomena, we stand a chance of not only knowing in part what she might represent but, more so, experiencing the healing force she embodies in our time.

Much has been said about our modern society being far too rational and masculine in its behavior and view of life. Because I believe this to be fundamentally true, it is necessary to point out that I am not writing as a male on behalf of woman, but as one person who happens to be male who is growing increasingly fatigued and weighed down with this cultural lopsidedness, which has distorted not only our understanding of the feminine, but of the masculine as well. One of the difficulties I have encountered in many attempts today to make room for the feminine is that they are made according to masculine guidelines and definitions, and this on the part of men and women alike. The feminine is all too often still forced to dance her seductive dance before our masculine view of things rather than dance her own dance, and in the end herself rejoice for our rejoicing. We repeatedly glorify her according to our biases, and so dig ourselves still deeper into our lopsidedness.

The dark feminine resists all attempts at idealization. Like the masculine, the feminine is archetypal, and it is the dark side of this archetype that alerts us to its autonomy. In the end both the masculine and the feminine are sacred mysteries. In terms of myth, we are speaking here of the gods and goddesses, unknowable but ever-present.

It is my belief that the dark feminine as incarnated in such places as Einsiedeln represents a phenomenon that transcends local boundaries and relates to Western spirituality in general. The psy-

---

* Throughout this work, the Black Madonna will be referred to with the personal pronouns "she" or "her." In no way should this be understood in a literal manner. The Black Madonna is archetypal, and in that sense impersonal. The formula has been adopted for literary convenience alone.

chological force behind her—the dark nature of the feminine—is clearly seen not only by those who stand before her at Einsiedeln but also by those who do not know her name, yet clearly feel her effect within them. An analysand once told me that her ten-year-old son said he knew how people could start seeing God in a new way. "How?" his mother asked, to which her son replied, "As a woman and black." A similar reflex to balance the the lopsidedness is evident in a minor anecdote involving the space program. An astronaut, upon returning from outer space, was asked by a cynical reporter if he had seen God out there. The astronaut answered, "Yes, and She's black." Such responses are not accidental, but reflect the need of the soul to individually and collectively balance itself. Again, in the movie "O God," the befuddled protagonist finds himself chosen by God to remind the world of His message. One day when the man (played by John Denver) is working at the grocery store, God appears to him and they begin talking. The conversation becomes heated, and to the protagonist's embarrassment a woman walks into their aisle; he turns to the customer to explain that this is indeed God and, turning back to point God out to the lady, discovers that God is now a hefty black woman.

Archetypal material is not possible to explain with a this or that response. Such material reveals itself through symbolic imagery in everyday life throughout individual and collective history. The Black Madonna of Einsiedeln is not just an isolated entity, but carries a religious and psychological significance with archetypal grounding. She is one of about four hundred other Black Madonnas throughout the world. Most renowned among these are Our Lady of Czestochowa in Jasna Gora, Poland, and Notre Dame de Monserrat in Spain. These Black Madonnas speak to that very deprived area of the soul which hungers for value and hope in the midst of the indefinition and incomprehensibility of life. Each is unique among her white counterparts. Each of these Black Madonnas carries the missing dark pole of the feminine archetype in our times.

It is possible to look at the Black Madonna in relation to several great goddesses in world religions, namely Kali of India, Hecate and Medusa of the Greeks, Isis of Egypt, as well as the ancient moon mysteries involving the feminine, the Eleusinian rites so essential to the Greeks, and to a great extent the alchemy of the Middle Ages. Such a grounding gives her spiritual and psychological substance, and thus raises her to a level of importance and significance for the modern Western mind—an import that ought not be ignored. It is my hope that as she is enriched through such amplification, the Black Madonna will take on clearer focus regarding her value for the spiritual maturity of the Western world.

In North America there is very little knowledge or living experience of the Black Madonna phenomenon. Our Lady of Guadalupe in Mexico is the closest we come, geographically and spiritually. The long evolution that produces a Black Madonna like the one at Einsiedeln has just not yet happened on North American soil. As will be seen, however, the archetypal roots of the dark feminine have already manifested in our history and are emerging ever more consciously in our individual and collective lives. Yet the dark feminine is rooted in the American soil itself, insofar as she represents the bounty and in particular the wisdom of the land. Native American cultures have traditionally understood this, as have many indigenous peoples bound to the land by complex systems of ritual and attitude. There is, however, no call for sentimentality or idealizing when speaking of the dark feminine, for what she represents is at once beautiful and potentially horrifying. The traditional Native American knows this intuitively, the relationship between the giving and the taking, the coming and the going, the nurturing and the murderous.

Western culture, in its often unthinking pervasiveness, has by nature separated and alienated us from the earth. Understanding and integrating the dark feminine puts us back in relation to the earth and all its life. This should be no great discovery, technically speaking—yet it is a vital one to modern humanity, which has long since lost that connection. The dark feminine is fascinating to us, who have collectively demythologized the land, and who have hence relegated the dark unknown to the unconscious, where it lives on merrily in our dreams and consulting rooms. Yet the feminine is just as much an external figure, in our land and history, as she is in our imaginations.

One very fine representation of this archetype, however, is located at the entrance/exit area of the San Francisco International Airport (see figure one). This modern sculpture by Beniamino Benvenuto (Benny Bufano) is of the Black Mother standing over St. Francis, who has four eyes symbolizing his ability to fully see— both heavenly and earthly, as well as in the four directions of life. The title of the sculpture is "Peace."

The Black Madonna of Einsiedeln—and her thousand-year history—provides us with a rich insight into the mysteries of the dark feminine. In looking specifically at *this* Black Virgin, it might be possible to glean a more general understanding of the archetype itself. Thus this study will constantly move from the particular to the universal, with frequent reference to case material and psychological reflection. The Black Madonna will be used as a touchstone in our understanding the archetypal dark feminine.

Throughout, it is my intention to give not only a psychological interpretation, but also a psychological perspective. It is my hope that, in a respectful way, this work will bring to light and enrich, on a deeper level of the psyche, the spiritual value which this Black Madonna embodies and which cannot, in the end, be ignored.

1

THE DARK FORCE AND THE RAVEN: THE JOURNEY WITHIN

The Black Madonna of Einsiedeln is the result of over eleven hundred years of history. She must not be seen as an object distinct from her history and the history of the present Einsiedeln Abbey. Her history is archetypal in that it has not simply yielded to the arbitrary forces of chance, but rather has always seemed to produce in its wake evidence of intentionality behind those seemingly independent happenings. This "intention" is related to the archetypal current in which history so often courses. Yet even if one does say that within those eleven hundred years there were nothing but isolated *historical* incidents, what then do we say to the fact that today many of those incidents are actively celebrated and venerated by thousands?

The present monastery—and consequently the Black Madonna herself—has its historical roots in the life and legend of its founder, St. Meginrat, or Meinrad, to use the later form of the name, who was born in Southern Swabia at Sulchen, the castle of his maternal ancestors, in approximately A.D.797, during the late years of Charlemagne's reign.[1] He belonged to the family of the Counts of Hohenzollern. His father, Count Berchtold von

1

Sulgen,[2] sent him to the then-famous school at the Abbey of Reichenau, situated on an island in the Untersee. Meinrad was ordained a priest, assuming the Benedictine habit in the year 822, at the age of twenty-five; he remained there for several years, illuminating Scripture. Both scholarly and conscientious, he was eventually sent to be a teacher at Benken on the upper Lake Zürich, where the Benedictines of Reichenau had established a school. Though an influential and gifted person, both in terms of scholarship and the business affairs of the monastery, he increasingly began to desire solitude. His first attempt to retreat was on the slopes of the Etzel mountain on the other side of Lake Zürich, in the year 828. He was thirty-one at this time. He lived there for seven years, praying and fasting. People came to hear him preach and to worship at the altar in his self-made hermitage. Desiring still greater solitude, he withdrew deeper into the Finsterwald, a forest across the Sihl River, taking with him the rule of St. Benedict, a missal, a book of homilies, the works of the Monk Cassian, and a statue of the Blessed Virgin presented to him by Abbess Hildegarde of Zürich. At this point he was thirty-eight years old.

According to the story, as Meinrad made his way into the Finsterwald he noticed a nest in a fir tree, above which two hawks were hovering threateningly.[3] The hermit chased the hawks away, climbed the tree, saved two ravens, and fed and cared for them. Finding a suitable clearing, he built a cell and a little chapel beside it. Meinrad dedicated the chapel to the Mother of God; today this is the site of the Monastery of Einsiedeln. The ravens stayed with him at his new hermitage.[4]

It is said that during his time at Einsiedeln, Meinrad experienced a dramatic encounter with a host of demons.[5] One day, while he was praying, a multitude of demons spread around him from all sides in such a manner that he was not even able to see the light of day. Terrified by these *tenebrarum ministris*, or servants of darkness, he prostrated himself on the ground in prayer and commended himself to God. After a long time, he saw a light in the

east, and then an angel following it. The angel came toward where
he was lying on the ground in prayer and entered into the midst
of the evil spirits. The angel commanded with great authority that
this group of demons go away. After they had dispersed, the angel consoled him and later departed. From that day onwards, St.
Meinrad did not have to face the terrors of such dark spirits.

Meinrad spent twenty-five years at Einsiedeln, until his death
on January 21, 861. The legend of his death goes as follows: early
one morning, while Meinrad was celebrating Mass, it was revealed
to him that his death would come that day; thieves were to come
and murder him. As his murderers-to-be made their way toward
Meinrad's cell, his ravens shot up into the air with such screech-
ing that the whole forest burst into commotion. The legend continues that Meinrad greeted the two men graciously, giving them
food and clothes. He said, "When you have killed me—and I know
you have come to do that—light two candles and put one at my
head and the other at my feet."[6] The two men then clubbed
him to death, but before they could light the candles, the wicks
lit of their own accord, revealing to them that they had killed
a saint. They fled in fear, not stopping until they reached a tav-
ern in Zürich.

In the town of Wollerau at the edge of the Finsterwald lived
a carpenter. He saw the ravens swooping around the heads of the
murderers as they fled from the woods. Suspecting something
wrong, he sent his brother to follow the ravens and himself went
to Meinrad's cell to investigate. There he found the Saint dead.
Setting out after his brother, the carpenter found him outside a
local inn. Meinrad's murderers were inside, believing themselves
finally safe. The ravens revealed their secret, however, by flying
in, knocking over their steins and pecking at their heads.

The two men were subsequently tried, convicted and condemned to death.[7] The two birds made their way onto the
monastery's coat of arms (see figure two). The psychological im-
plications of the St. Meinrad legend lay the foundation out of
which the Black Madonna later emerged.

It might be asked just why St. Meinrad wanted to become a hermit. An answer can be formulated in terms of how he spent the first part of his life, as opposed to his later years. Here it must not be forgotten that he was born into an aristocratic family of the Counts of Hohenzollern, that he was ordained a priest and served in the established monastery at Reichenau. In every respect, it seems likely that he was a product of his culture. Situated on a main tributary of the Rhine, Reichenau embodied the essence of that culture. Meinrad's move away from this area, and later from the small school near Benken on Lake Zürich, clearly reflects his need to retreat from the familiar and known. How true this was is pointed out by his move from his first hermitage at Etzel to his final one at Einsiedeln. He did not find the solitude he needed at the Etzel location, for he was constantly visited by people from the surrounding area. Not only did he seek refuge from cultural influences, he did not even want members of that culture to visit him. It must be noted that he was thirty-eight years old when he moved to Einsiedeln, and that this is very often a turning point in one's spiritual life, a time when one's personal goals lie behind; newer and deeper issues must be faced in order that life have a more grounded and durable meaning.

The Finsterwald represented this needed solitude. It is hard for us to imagine what such a place would look like to someone over a thousand years ago. It was indeed what its name implies. *Finster* is a German word meaning obscure, dark, gloomy, and somber. It was not, like Reichenau, a center of scholarship and commerce, or a place of laws and customs. Rather it was a place of uncertainties, of natural laws that could be either hazardous or beneficial to whomever entered it. It was characterized by its unpredictable nature—a nature that one could not manipulate and change according to individual will, but which one had to submit to by listening to, observing, adjusting to, and ultimately respecting.

The forest in general represents a region closer to the human world than, say, a desert or a body of water, which like the forest

are metaphors of the unknown. The forest has long figured as
the starting point of a hero's adventures. According to Emma Jung
and Marie-Louise von Franz,

> In many fairy-tales and poems the forest is the starting point for
> the journeyings and deeds of the hero. This represents the emer-
> gence from a relatively unconscious situation into a far more con-
> scious one.[8]

It was here that Meinrad began his heroic journey. In Arthuri-
an legend the forest is often the place of supernatural beings and
wonders, or else the way to them often lies through a forest. In
a fourteenth-century poem, *Sir Gawain and the Green Knight*, the
knight Gawain reaches the hall of the Green Knight after riding
through a forest. The path that leads to the hall is roofed on either side with tall trees, creating a dark and eerie passage. Dante's
Inferno begins in a gloomy wooded area; the Celtic druids worshipped and lived in the forest and saw it as a natural sanctuary.
Whether mysterious and dark or providing shelter, the forest has
a cathedral-like majesty that can convey a sense of the presence
of the divine.[9] Meinrad brought with him the statue of the Virgin Mother and made her the center around which his hermitage
grew. Today she still figures as the "Madonna in the Finsterwald."

Circe's house in the *Odyssey* is but one of many other examples
of the forest providing a home for the dark feminine. In the fairy
tale of Hansel and Gretel, she takes the form of a cannibalistic
witch. Frau Trude, a German fairy tale character, lives in the forest; the Russian story of Baba Yaga is also about a woman who
lives in a hut in a forest clearing, a hut surrounded by a fence
topped by skulls. Though obviously destructive (she cooks and
eats children), Baba Yaga also guards the fountain of the water
of life.

The dark feminine and the forest are closely associated not only
in literature, but also psychologically. The following dream, for
example, is from a man in his early forties who was struggling
to understand his life in the context of a recent tragedy:

Members of a dream group I am a part of and a few others, whom I cannot identify as anyone I know, are playing in thick woods crisscrossed by narrow paths. We aren't blindfolded and it's daytime, but the woods are so dark that we cannot see anyone else until we are right next to them. In a mood of playful searching, as in a game of blindman's bluff, we keep finding each other on the paths, and then after a hearty greeting and laugh, we quickly separate in a kind of regular rhythm, as in a dance. One of the people I don't know is a black woman who seems to dominate the entire proceedings with her presence and her almost constant, ringing laugh.

A year prior to this dream, the individual's wife died in a plane crash. Already an introspective and insightful man, this tragedy threw him even deeper into his own life journey. He joined a group of people who valued and studied their dreams systematically. This dream picks up on this search and describes woods very much like the Finsterwald—"so dark that we cannot see anyone else until we are right next to them." There is ambiguity in the dream, for in the midst of the darkness there is play, dance and laughter. There is an inner order to the thick woods in that it is crisscrossed by narrow paths. The characters are hiding, seeking, finding, and again separating with a "kind of regular rhythm, as in a dance." Throughout it all is the ringing laughter of the black woman who "dominates the entire proceedings with her presence." The dream reflects the man's continued search within himself and, at the same time, lifts the darkness beyond his personal tragedy. In the dream, dark woods and the black woman go together and impressively portray the healing power within this man's soul.

The theme of the woman and the forest can express itself both positively or negatively, just as Baba Yaga is both destructive yet harbors the source of living waters. Again, in the words of Jung and von Franz, "Understood as protecting and nourishing nature, the forest also represents the all-embracing quality of the mother. . ."[10] At the same time, this maternal symbol has a dual nature, for the forest is not only the place of growth and life, but also of death and decay. Both are part of the natural cycle of life.

The forest destroys as it gives life. It is the refuge of saints and sinners, of all who stand outside or are at odds with the conscious realm. It is the home of robbers, thieves, hermits, spirits, dragons, and witches. It is the magic realm of wonderful and terrifying events. In short, the forest symbolizes the unknown component of the psyche. According to C. G. Jung,

> The forest, dark and impenetrable to the eye, like deep water and the sea, is the container of the unknown and the mysterious. It is an appropriate synonym for the unconscious."

Thus the Finsterwald is clearly a symbol for the unconscious, harboring all possibilities. Like the unconscious, it presents not only dangers but also the opportunity for change and renewal.

This association of the Black Madonna and the woods was most impressively echoed in the dream of a forty-one year old woman whom we will call Anna. I will present the dream in its entirety.

> My husband, son and I were trying out new cars. My husband had brought two along so we could find out which one would suit us best. There was a regular yellow car and a very special green jeep which was unusual in that it could be adjusted in many different ways to suit different situations. We decided that the jeep was just right for us and to buy it. We tried the cars out in a place called "Holy Hill." This was a hill or mountain on which was built a sanctuary of the Blessed Mother. The church was big and completely white. It was a holy place to which many pilgrims came to venerate the Blessed Mother. Priests and monks took care of it. My husband and son returned the yellow car, and I was left with the jeep. I tried it out on the road by the Great White Church. I was scared at first when I tried to handle it, but it was all right.
>
> I then left the car and entered the sanctuary. When I got inside, I suddenly knew that my paintings of the suffering black goddess were very important. I knew that this was the place for which I was to paint them, I saw that my pictures would be brought into this church and hung there for the pilgrims to see and contemplate.
>
> There was another church in a nearby city, and I understood that I had to make pictures for that church too. These were also to be pictures of the suffering black Madonna. I had these pic-

tures all in my mind and was carrying them around in my heart. I saw them all with my inner eyes. I understood how important it was to paint them and to exhibit them in these churches. People would come and look at them and love them.

Contrary to what it might seem, Anna was not suffering an inflation, nor was the dream compensating for an inferior attitude. Anna was a first-generation German immigrant who as a child had experienced the chaos of the Second World War. She came from a strict and sober Roman Catholic family. During analysis she began dreaming repeatedly of a black woman and experiencing her in active imagination (the process of allowing the unconscious to come up into consciousness, where the ego will relate to or enter into dialogue with what is experienced). Anna was a talented artist, but had not taken the opportunity to develop her ability. This dream indeed lifts her up to the level of her ability and presents her with a religious vocation of sorts entailing collective responsibilities (i.e., . . ."my pictures would be brought into this Church and hung there for the pilgrims to see and contemplate"), which is not uncommon in truly artistic individuals.

Holy Hill actually is a pilgrim site which this dreamer knew of and which is located in a wooded area on a hill. It also serves as a religious reflection of her own inner center—a center experienced consciously up to this point in an all-too-white a manner ("the Church was completely white"). It is as though her inner world knew that a balance needed to be struck in her religious outlook. In fact she had completely rejected her Roman Catholic background because of its apparent sterility. Through her growing relationship, in dreams and active imagination, with the "suffering black goddess," she once again found enthusiasm and direction for her own religious life.

Meinrad also experienced such a need for a change in his own life when he chose to enter the Finsterwald. Psychologically speaking, the movement is from a solid conscious position to the unpredictable, uncertain nature of the unconscious psyche, a classic example of introversion for the sake of renewal. Meinrad's actual move from Reichenau to the monastery near Benken, to Etzel, and finally deep into the Finsterwald, paralleled what must have been his own inner need to move into the unknown, dark, uncertain side of his unconscious psyche. Even at this stage, the Black Madonna is anticipated in the guise of the Finsterwald, for the forest was *her* in her primitive undifferentiated state: the *prima materia*, the beginning substance from which the subsequent historical treasures were to be redeemed.

As is the case with the individual psyche, one's initial contact with the unconscious is like going into an uncertain, unpredictable wilderness. It is a journey into the dark maternal depths, with all of the fears and expectations it entails. It is a submission of the ego to the vital messages of the unconscious. On a psychological level, the descent into the unconscious involves abandoning the immediate demands of one's ego in favor of coming into contact with one's deeper psyche, whose ultimate goal is individual wholeness. The original function of ritual fasting was spiritual (psychic) purification; through fasting, one prepares oneself for communion with God by, according to the encyclopedia *Man, Myth and Magic*, "heightening the mental faculties and increasing spiritual receptivity."[12] In effect, it is a means of cleansing the conscious domain by ridding it of the interference of the conscious ego. Through fasting or prayer, one becomes more receptive to the voices within.

Such discipline is invaluable in bringing one to a conscious sensitivity to the issues of life and death. In his confrontation with the host of demons, Meinrad thus did the only possible thing— he prostrated himself before the awful company. Such visitations are not uncommon to saints and religious personalities. Indeed they seem to be necessary, perhaps even the precondition for any deep spiritual growth and insight. Full spiritual development necessitates an experience with the dark side of life, which pushes back superficial responses and makes room for balance, understanding and compassion. One is reminded of Jesus's encounter with Satan in the wilderness, (Mt. 4:1-11, Mk. 1:12-13, Lk. 4:1-13). He

too had to face evil and tremendous temptation before he could
go on with his ministry. In the end, angels came and ministered
to him as one came and ministered to Meinrad. To be isolated
in a spirit-infested place like the Finsterwald would certainly in-
tensify such an experience. But more basic than this is the inner
psychological necessity that demands one to face the issue of evil
in its more frightening and threatening aspects before any further growth can take place—the need to face even that evil which
cannot be reduced to a logical explanation nor traced to some
causal relationship. Meinrad and Christ symbolize our need to
face evil as it exists in an absolute sense—in and of itself and de-
pendent on no outside agent.

The dark, shadowy, unknown side of St. Meinrad's psyche is
certainly in evidence in this confrontation with the demons. When
a person withdraws as Meinrad did, he (or she) is bound to experience an excess of psychic energy, which strengthens the autonomous complexes of the unconscious. This can produce what we
call hallucinations, or lend impetus to what is otherwise known
as a mystical vision or experience. The appearance of such complexes is usually unpleasant." Yet Meinrad's demons seem more
than mere projected manifestations of his own personal dark side;
rather, they seem to show how evil can manifest itself impersonally,
or threaten impersonally by forces that seem to originate from
without. In truth, such evil is one aspect of the unconscious. To
lie prostrate in the midst of such a host—a truly depressing
experience—is to admit to one's helplessness.

But to pray to God for help is an appeal to a peaceful center
within the turmoil. It is a cry and at the same time a striving
toward orientation in the midst of chaos; we often experience it
as hope. For Meinrad it is this hope that shines through and ultimately disperses the awful crowd. Angels are figures of light—
Bunyan called them "Shining Ones."" The messengers of God,
in psychological terms they signify the messengers of that inner
psychic center Jung called the Self. They are psychic contents,
and the vehicle or means by which this inner Self can manifest

itself in special situations. Accordingly, it is not uncommon for
the Self or God to appear in times of great duress and helplessness.

When the ego surrenders, more powerful forces and deeper
values can be reached. That Meinrad was not harassed by demons
after the visitation is consistent with the lasting impression such
an experience can make on a person—it is in fact a touchstone
that guides one the rest of one's life. For those who experienced
and survived Dachau, there is no need to re-experience evil.

To become a hermit psychologically implies not so much a physical separation from mankind as a turning inward to concentrate
on the psychic mysteries that can assist a person seeking a more
wholesome meaning for himself. This was Meinrad's need and
the need of many people who seek those values in life not immediately accessible to the conscious mind. For these individuals, as for Meinrad, the dark aspect of the unconscious, the
Schwarzemuttergottes (The Black Mother of God) in her initial undeveloped stage, the Finsterwald, or whatever other name captures this experience, becomes the ground for a more mature
spiritual development.

In terms of Meinrad's personal psychology, and more impor-
tantly, in terms of a much more universal psychological dynamic, the Finsterwald is the *prima materia*, the undeveloped and
undifferentiated psychic material that had to be transformed by
Meinrad's introspective journey. The forest represents elements
of the *Schwarzemuttergottes* that have yet to be made conscious
and valued by the ego. This dynamic is repeatedly underscored
in the legend, especially by the relationship between Meinrad and
the two ravens that he rescues from the talons of a hawk.

While both the raven and the hawk are technically considered,
in almost every dictionary of symbols, to represent thoughts, or
the process of thinking, in terms of the legend there is a very sharp
distinction between what each type of bird represents. In the Egyptian myth of Horus's sparrow-hawk, as well as in the myths and
symbolism of the Graeco-Roman age,[15] the hawk is very
definitely associated with the sun—that is, with the patriarchal

values of logic and linear thinking. The raven, on the other hand, traditionally represents only the darker aspects, the shadow, of consciousness. That the hawk would thus descend upon the young ravens symbolically represents the hostility of consciousness towards contents of the unconscious, especially embryonic contents—such as new awareness of attitudes or opinions—that need to be nourished and cared for.

Meinrad's rescue of the ravens is a spiritual victory for the emerging unconscious. The Finsterwald and the two ravens are closely related, one being the *prima materia* of the unconscious, the other, one's personal relationship to the contents that begin to arise from it. Meinrad could have left the ravens to the hawk. That he did not reflects his attitude toward the unknown, the dark mysterious aspect of life which can all too easily be displaced by the kind of scholastic training and cultural background available to Meinrad.

It is interesting here to note that in alchemy—which Jung has showed to be a highly developed psychological metaphor for the process of individuation—"great importance was attached to the blackness as the starting point of the [alchemical] work. Generally it was called the 'Raven'."[16] The entry of Meinrad into the Finsterwald and the rescue of the ravens is indeed the starting point of a great work that developed into the cult of Mary, and which later emphasized her blackness. One can either turn from this *nigredo* ("blackening," in alchemical Latin), or face it in expectation and sacrifice. The rescue of the ravens reflects Meinrad's willingness to face it. As a symbol of the *nigredo*, the raven is highly complex and ambiguous. According to Jung,

> It is of the essence of the transforming substance to be on the one hand extremely common, even contemptible (this is expressed in the series of attributes it shares with the devil, such as serpent, dragon, raven, lion, basilisk, and eagle), but on the other hand to mean something of great value, not to say divine. For the transformation leads from the depths to the heights, from the bestially archaic and infantile to the mystical *homo maximus*.[17]

Elsewhere, Jung tells us that "*Corvus* (crow or raven) or *caput corvi* (raven's head) is the traditional name for the *nigredo* (nox, melancholia, etc.)"[18] To nourish the ravens is to nourish the contents from the dark experiences of one's psyche and life, to keep them alive and constantly in mind. The chthonic secrets of life represented by the ravens can thus be understood as the source of Meinrad's later wisdom, insight, and holiness.

The raven can represent the unofficial thoughts of God, and thus become messengers of the darker unknown and less visible side of Himself.[19] According to von Franz,

> The raven might lead either to possession by evil or into essential inner realizations which are always the dark side of the sun God, i.e., thoughts not dominant in collective consciousness at the moment, which the collective would look upon as evil.[20]

Ravens are indeed worthy and appropriate companions for St. Meinrad in that they fulfill their traditional role as messengers of the gods, i.e., carriers of the vital messages of the unconscious to consciousness.[21]

Meinrad's pursuit of a deeper meaning in life had to go the way of the *nigredo*, the black Finsterwald. As Jung expresses it in the *Mysterium Coniunctionis*, his study in the psychology of alchemy,

> Self-knowledge is an adventure that carries us unexpectedly far and deep. Even a moderately comprehensive knowledge of the shadow can cause a good deal of confusion and mental darkness, since it gives rise to personality problems which one had never remotely imagined before. For this reason alone, we can understand why the alchemists called their *nigredo* melancholia, "a black blacker than black," night, an affliction of the soul, confusion, etc., or, more pointedly, the "black raven." For us the raven seems only a funny allegory, but for the medieval adept it was, as we have said, a well-known allegory of the devil.[22]

Here is where the ambiguous nature of the raven is most pronounced. For though Meinrad *had* to rescue the ravens as a prerequisite for his beginning the individuation process, the ravens in turn were the heralds of his death, though themselves innocent of it. In one respect, it might be said that Meinrad's rescue and tending of the ravens is another way of showing his willingness to accept his own death. A parallel can be found in the *Mysterium Coniunctionis*, where Jung quotes a section from the alchemical tract *Introitus apertus* : "With the death of the lion the raven is born, i.e., when desire dies, the blackness of death sets in."[23] The passage seems to have some bearing on Meinrad's case. The sacrifice of consciousness calls for its death and the entry of the dark strength of the unconscious. For a transformation to take place, the old personality must die. The old Meinrad must change if there is to be a renewal. His death metaphorically expresses the universal need for one to contact the dark side of the unconscious before one can find the opportunity for renewal. This renewal and restoration motif is, as will be seen later, crucial to the development of the Black Madonna, and specifically to her Einsiedeln shrine.

The murder of St. Meinrad takes on an interesting twist as it is portrayed in a twelfth-century miniature, Cod. 111 of Einsiedeln Library (figure three). Meinrad is shown kneeling between his two murderers, who are in the act of clubbing him to death. From the heavens, an angel reaches down in a gesture of blessing and acceptance. Variations on this theme are relatively common in mythology. In depictions of the Mithraic bull sacrifice, Cautes and Cautopates are shown one with a raised and the other with a lowered torch. There is a parallel with the Christian sacrifice — Christ on the cross flanked by two thieves, one of whom ascends to heaven and the other descends to hell. In both cases, there is a vital relationship between the sacrificed and the two attendants. According to Jung, "the two thieves somehow go together with Christ."[24] The reference here is to the immortal and mortal aspects of the psyche. Thus just as Mithras, Cautes and Cautopates, as well as Christ and the two thieves, form two different personalities with three different aspects to each personality, Meinrad and his two murderers seem to reflect one personality.[25]

This twelfth-century image shows one murderer raised above the other, suggesting the presence of a psychic hierarchy—a higher and a lower nature. Though the immortal aspect is usually expressed through one of the attendants, it is here seen in the angelic blessing and acceptance. The murderers are themselves representatives of the dark destroying elements of the unconscious, an inherent destructiveness that certainly can be characterized as evil by the conscious mind, but without which no higher transformation could take place. Psychologically, what the image is calling for is a complete submission to the unconscious.

It is not uncommon in therapy to encounter dreams or fantasies of dying. These frequently represent a need for renewal, and they demand that the ego surrender something in order for the transformation to begin. Dreams of execution, of being cut up, beaten, or murdered, or even fantasies of suicide, all in some way or other raise the theme of a need for renewal. Something needs to die in order that something new can emerge. It often happens that the more unconscious or resistant an individual is to this need, the more horrific and bloody these images will be. The thieves thus play a significant role in Meinrad's transformation, since they can be understood as emblems of his own psychic renunciation—a supposition borne out by his willing acceptance of death at their hands, and especially by the kindness and serenity he displays towards them. They are his awful means of transformation, the instruments of his death, but a necessity in itself if renewal is to take place; for

> . . .the Christian idea of sacrifice is symbolized by the death of a human being and demands a surrender of the whole man—not merely a taming of his animal instincts, but a total renunciation of them and a disciplining of his specifically human, spiritual functions for the sake of a spiritual goal beyond this world.[26]

The measure of Meinrad's achievement is graphically expressed in the miraculous lighting of the two candles, one at his head and one at his feet. This seems to serve as a sign that his life's task was successful. That the candles would be so placed once again alludes to the mutual co-existence of a higher and lower nature (conscious and unconscious), a major theme in his biography. The miraculous lighting is really a variation on the motif that fire was originally the sole possession of the gods. That it should here represent divine intercession is highly significant. On the purely psychological level, it means that the center of the personality, what Jung would call the Self, bestows psychic energy in a way that harmoniously balances the poles of the conscious and unconscious. The candle itself suggests such an individuating principle—since, according to Cirlot's *Dictionary of Symbols*,

> like the lamp, [the candle] is a symbol of individuated light, and consequently of the life of an individual as opposed to the cosmic and universal life.[27]

In Christian tradition, two candles are customarily placed on an altar to signify the dual nature of Christ as both Son of Man and Son of God. Both burn equally bright. In short, the discovery of fire was metaphorically a discovery of one's inner divine spark as well, thus pointing toward not only the wonder of the external fire, but also of its equivalent symbolic form within the psyche. The giving of fire as in Meinrad's legend strongly reminds us that fire, that is, psychic energy, has been bestowed in a most beneficial way and that, in the end, it is not our sole or full possession, but a property of our total personality which comes from a source far beyond our conscious understanding.

The life and legend of St. Meinrad set the stage for a fuller appreciation of the Einsiedeln Black Madonna phenomenon, since the two are inextricably linked both historically and psychologically. The Finsterwald and the Black Madonna represent many of the same elements in psychic terms; both are fundamentally maternal, and both are literally and figuratively dark (i.e., associated with unconscious contents).

The link between Meinrad and the Black Madonna is underscored in the history and liturgical tradition of the Einsiedeln monastery as well. For instance, to this day Meinrad's skull is kept in a small casket on the altar near the feet of the Black Madonna. On the eighth day (the octave) after the annual Pontifical High Mass held on the anniversary of Meinrad's death (January 21), the same ceremonies are held in the Lady Chapel housing the Black Madonna. Before Vespers, a blessing is given with the saint's head.[28]

A final link is that the Black Madonna draws her sobriquet ("Our Lady of Hermits") from the style of Meinrad's life and the example of those who followed him; Einsiedeln means "The Hermitage." *Meginratescella* (St. Meinrad's Cell) is the oldest name for Einsiedeln.[29] From that cell developed a center of monastic life focused on the Black Madonna. Maria-Einsiedeln is not only a name, but a testimony to the relationship that has always existed between the hermit and the Virgin Mother.

Chapter One Notes

[1]Unless otherwise noted, general information concerning the life of
St. Meinrad is taken from the following sources:
Bennett, *Einsiedeln "In the Dark Wood,"* 1883
Raeber, "Our Lady of the Hermits" (guidebook), 1972
Hengeller, "Brief Guide to the Abbey of Our Lady of the
Hermits," no date

[2]Helbling, *Das Blockbuch von Sankt Meinrad und Seinen Moedern und
von Ursprung von Einsiedeln,* p. 11. The first reports state that Meinrad's parents lived in Suelich, not Sulgen, Sulgau or Saulgau.

[3]Müller-Guggenbühl, *Swiss-Alpine Folk-Tales,* pp. 205-209

[4]For a more detailed account of the life of St. Meinrad, see the Bib-
liography to the *Professbuch der Benediktinerabtei Einsiedeln,* by
Rudolf Henngeler, Einsiedeln, 1933

[5]From *Vita S. Meginrati,* O. Holder-Egger, Ed. MG, SS XV, 455ss in
the Einsiedeln library

[6]*Swiss-Alpine Folk-Tales,* p. 207

[7]The *Blockbuch von Sankt Meinrad* says that these two murderers were
named Peter and Richart, and that the raven not only hacked at
their heads but continued to do so until they died. Other depictions show the murderers, though dead, being taken away to have
their bones crushed under a huge wagon wheel, then themselves
being tied to the wheel and burned. Their ashes were then thrown
into the water (p. 18ff)

[8]E. Jung and M.-L. von Franz, *The Grail Legend,* p. 39ff

[9]*Dictionnaire des symboles,* pp. 366-367

[10]Jung-von Franz, p. 39

[11]C.G. Jung, *CW* XIII, p. 194

[12]*Man, Myth and Magic,* Vol. III, p. 917

[13]Von Franz, *Shadow and Evil in Fairytales,* p. 151

[14]*Man, Myth and Magic,* Vol. I, p.88

[15]*Ibid.,* Vol. III, p.1227

[16]C.G. Jung, *CW* XIV, p. 512

[17]C.G. Jung, *CW* XII, p. 134

[18]C.G. Jung, *CW* XIV, p. 510

[19]von Franz, p. 212

[20]*Ibid.*

[21]In Germanic mythology, Odin's two ravens also went forth each day to see what was happening, and returned to perch on his shoulders and whisper their news into his ears. Odin's ravens were named Huginn and Muninn, or "Thought" and "Memory"

[22]C.G. Jung, *CW* XIV, pp. 520-521

[23]*Ibid.*, p. 516n

[24]C.G. Jung, *CW* V, p. 201

[25]*Ibid.*, pp. 200-201

[26]*Ibid.*, p. 435

[27]*A Dictionary of Symbols*, p. 36

[28]Baeber, *Our Lady of Hermits*, pp. 34-35

[29]*Ibid.*, p. 7

2

THE HISTORICAL REFINEMENT IN THE EMERGENCE OF THE BLACK MADONNA

Between the time St. Meinrad built his cell in a Finsterwald clearing and the time when the cornerstone of the present monastery was laid (March 31, 1704), nine centuries passed. These were years that saw the repeated destruction and renewal of the shrine, each instance of which contributed to the process of refinement and evolution that gave structure and meaning to the Finsterwald legend; this in turn is linked to the transformation of the Einsiedeln Black Madonna, a long and arduous process culminating in her present-day role as spiritual shrine and center of pilgrimage.

Seventy-four years after Meinrad's death, St. Benno—of a princely Burgundian house, and a Canon of the Cathedral of Strasbourg—went with some of his friends to live at the hermitage of St. Meinrad. The cells they built encircled the Holy Chapel of Meinrad. He lived there until 925, when he was elevated to the See of Metz. Unfortunately, a short time afterwards enemies rose up against him, dragged him from his palace, tore out his eyes and banished him. The then-king of Germany condemned the offenders to death and invited St. Benno to return to his dio-

21

cese. He preferred, however, to return to his cell and companions at Einsiedeln, where he remained until his death in 940.

The Hermitage had an alluring call on such men as St. Benno, who like Meinrad was a nobleman and well respected in the Church. The early work of Meinrad was already being celebrated, as can be seen by the fact that the monastic cells were built around the chapel he had built for the Virgin Mother. The chapel became the center and focus of early monastic life at Einsiedeln.

When Eberhard, a French nobleman, came to Einsiedeln in 934 (St. Benno was still alive), he drew up plans for a church and a large monastery to be built on the spot where Meinrad died. The interesting feature here is that the chapel built by Meinrad was to remain on the same site, while the walls of the Church itself were to be built above and around it. This same style survives today at Einsiedeln, where the Lady Chapel is situated inside the huge cathedral.

The architectural configuration of the Einsiedeln monastery can be theologically understood as allowing the Virgin Mother to act as a center from which a more inclusive understanding of the God-head can be reached. In effect, she made the idea of a trinitarian masculine godhead more palatable to the individual psyche by softening it (this dynamic will be more closely studied in later chapters), by placing herself in a complementary though unassuming relationship with it, and thus adding another dimension to the prevailing and decidedly rationalistic and doctrinary understanding of God.

This need to balance the overly patriarchal Trinity may not be obvious, but expresses itself in the unconscious dreams and fantasies of many individuals today. Sometimes such unconscious material will go unnoticed; at other times it will feel quite unorthodox. A fifty-five year old woman, a married professional struggling with her religious views of herself and life that had for so long excluded the dark side, had the following dream:

There were two black women with gentle faces — good women. I know they can make the sign of the cross and dispel evil. I can't remember how to do it and feel anxious. But I say "in the name of the Father, Son and Holy Ghost" and the evil ones are powerless.

At first the dream seems innocent enough. This woman had a Christian background, but was at a point in her life when she wanted to look more deeply and consciously at the direction her life was taking, in particular questioning her religious beliefs. The dream shows that it was through the dark feminine side of her soul that she was able to deal with the power of the "evil ones." The dark side is not in basic opposition to the traditional view of the trinitarian godhead, but it is through the dark feminine that the dreamer is reminded and compelled to once again call on the triune God. This dream signals the return of the feminine as a vital part of this woman's spiritual journey.

Psychologically, the Black Madonna stands in the center of monastic life at Einsiedeln because she is the means of establishing a psychic balance and wholeness. The unconscious she represents becomes the means for developing such wholeness. In the patriarchal monastic setting, the opposite would be sure to be constellated in some form—whether by the need to enter the Finsterwald by making the Mother of God Chapel central, or simply by venerating a Black Madonna.

Eberhard went on to become the first Abbot of the Community, and he gave the monks the rule of St. Benedict. He placed the monastery under the protection of the Blessed Virgin, and chose "Our Lady of the Hermits" for its name. This then became the first concrete expression of Einsiedeln's initial relationship to the Virgin Mother—that is, she became ecclesiastically grounded and recognized. This was an important move, for it created a means by which the black aspect of the Madonna could become accepted and integrated into the Church.

It might seem that the blackness of the Madonna had disappeared by this time, for there is no evidence that the early statue of the Virgin was black. Yet an aspect of an archetype does not disappear into non-existence. It simply goes underground, into the unconscious, and may manifest itself in a disguised form, if at all. Earlier, I mentioned the strong possibility that the Black Madonna was first embodied, in a less conscious and more un-differentiated form, by the Finsterwald. Perhaps this undeveloped medium carried the dark half of the feminine archetype for many centuries, for it is hardly likely that the Finsterwald became less dark and gloomy just because of the monastery. It was still a dangerous place to enter, and thus it remained a most worthy hook upon which to hang the projections of the mysterious and capricious nature of the psyche. It is true, however, that the Monastery made the Finsterwald more approachable, while not necessarily negating its dangers. This is psychologically parallel to a man's encounter with the feminine side of his psyche. The feminine image (anima) in a man personifies the indeterminate and vague domain of the unconscious and, accordingly, can make it more approachable. The Virgin Mother represents the Finsterwald around her, and the spiritual searching of the pilgrims who came to her. However, as we will see later, the Madonna in her truly black form, not disguised in the Finsterwald or in any other manner, was to emerge before the conscious collective eye at Einsiedeln in a most remarkable way.

Eberhard asked Conrad, Bishop of Constance, to consecrate both the Holy Chapel and the church attached to the monastery. Bishop Conrad must have been a noted personality in his day, since he was canonized in the year 1123. He was Bishop from 934 until his death on November 26, 975. He is honored today, and the anniversary of his death (November 26) occupies an official place in the Church calendar.

The Bishop and his company arrived in Einsiedeln on September 14, 948, and the consecration was to take place the next day. On the day of his arrival, the Bishop went to the Holy Chapel to pray. Many of the ancient woodcut prints underscore the fact that it was night and that the stars were shining. It is said that as he prayed, the words of the Sixteenth Psalm came to him:

The Lord is my chosen portion and my cup; thou holdest my lot.
The lines have fallen for me in pleasant places; yea, I have a goodly
heritage. I bless the Lord who gives me counsel; in the night also
my heart instructs me.[1]

It is also said that he was there only a short time before the chapel was suddenly filled with "light brighter than that of the sun at midday, while the chanting of psalms by a great multitude fell upon his ears."[2] Going to the illuminated altar, he saw Jesus Christ Himself standing in front of the statue of the Virgin Mother. He was assisted by the four Evangelists, and was offering the Most Holy Sacrifice. Angels on either side of Jesus sent incense in the air while the apostles Peter and Paul and the Pope St. Gregory bore in their hands the Pontifical insignia. Saints Augustine and Ambrose were also assisting. A choir of angels sang while Saints Stephen and Lawrence officiated as deacons. In his legendary book *De secretis secretorum* (*On the Secrets of Secrets*), Bishop Conrad says that the text of the *Sanctus*, *Benedictus*, and *Agnus Dei* had been altered to read as follows:

Sanctus Deus, in aula gloriosae Virginis, miserere nobis. (Holy God in the realm of the Glorious Virgin, have mercy upon us).
Benedictus Mariae filius in aeternum regnaturus, qui venit in nomine domini. Hosanna in excelsis. (Blessed is the Son of Mary reigning in eternity, who comes in the name of the Lord. Hosanna in the highest).
Agnus Dei, qui tollis peccata mundi, miserere vivorum in te pie credentium.
Agnus Dei, qui tollis peccata mundi, miserere mortuorum, in te pie quiescentium.
Agnus Dei, qui tollis peccata mundi, da pacem vivis et defunctis in te pie regnantibus.
(Lamb of God, who takes away the sins of the world, have mercy upon the living who believe in you piously.
Lamb of God, who takes away the sins of the world, have mercy upon the dead who are resting in you piously.
Lamb of God, who takes away the sins of the world, give peace to the living and the dead who are reigning in you piously).

These are quite different from the original *Sanctus Deus, Benedictus,* and *Agnus Dei,* which read as follows:

Sanctus Sanctus Sanctus dominus Deus Sabaoth. Pleni sunt caeli gloria tua. (Holy Holy Holy Lord God of Sabaoth. The heavens are full of your glory).
Benedictus que venit in nomine Domini. Hosanna in excelsis. (Blessed is he who comes in the name of the Lord. Hosanna in the highest).
Agnus Dei, qui tollis peccata mundi: miserere nobis.
Agnus Dei, qui tollis peccata mundi: miserere nobis.
Agnus Dei, qui tollis peccata mundi: dona nobis pacem.
(Lamb of God, who takes away the sins of the world, have mercy upon us [repeated]. Lamb of God, who takes away the sins of the world, grant us thy peace).

These alterations are important, as they are still found in the liturgy of the monastery today. Records at the monastery say that St. Conrad told St. Eberhard what he had seen, but he was not believed. He did not want to consecrate a chapel that had already received a Divine Dedication. With great reservation, however, he finally returned to the church at dawn and prepared to ascend the steps leading to the altar in the Holy Chapel, when, as soon as he placed his foot upon the first step of the altar, a seemingly heaven-borne voice was heard by all present: "Cease, brother, the Chapel is divinely consecrated." *(Cessa, cessa, frater, Capella divinitus consecrata est).*

The first Divine Dedication of 948 may be historically questionable, other than that a dedication of some sort by St. Conrad did take place. In a private conversation in 1974, the then Rector, Father Ludwig Raeber, said that "The legend was the fruit of the pilgrims." It is interesting that several references attempt to ground the legend in history. Such sources say that in 964 the event was publicly declared to Pope Leo VIII, who reigned from 963 until his death in 965. St. Conrad was present, in addition to Emperor Otto and his wife Adelheid, as well as "many other personages, secular and ecclesiastic." The words attributed to Conrad are recorded in a small document, *Madonna im Finstern*

Wald, in which he testifies to the event as he saw and heard it.⁴ A papal bull was issued declaring "Anathema upon any who, in the future, would dare to renew the consecration of the Holy Chapel," and concluding with these words: "We absolve all who shall visit the above named holy spot, after confession and repentance from all their sins and the penalties attached thereto."⁵ The legend thus became a part of history, which in itself reveals the very important position this chapel occupied in the collective mind. In truth, the Holy Chapel changed from being the chapel dedicated *to* the Redeemer, as in the beginning, to that of a chapel dedicated *by* the Redeemer.

I personally prefer to approach this event from the standpoint of legend, since historicity is ultimately a peripheral issue. What is more significant is that the account was important enough to celebrate annually, and for the Church to issue a special Papal bull in commemoration of it. For whatever else can be said of the Divine Consecration, it is certain that a meaning of a highly archetypal nature surrounds it. It is safe to say that as the Holy Chapel became more and more important to the pilgrims, the need arose – perhaps simultaneously – to sanctify that place especially in the name of the Divine Mother. It increasingly became Her Chapel.

What is especially interesting here, however, is the unorthodox manner of the consecration. For example, the legend is emphatic in stating that the dedication did not take place on the intended day, September 15, but rather on the day before. The dedication did not take place in daylight in the presence of a host of people; rather, it took place at night, in the presence of only one, St. Conrad. Old woodcuts of this event in the library at Einsiedeln repeatedly show a night sky with shining stars. The artists made a point of adding a window to the prints to emphasize this fact. Conrad's reference to the Sixteenth Psalm is also interesting in this regard. Not only does he say, "I bless the Lord who gives me counsel" but, "in the night also my heart instructs me." The emphasis is on the night as against the day – which is custodian of the sun and thus closely related to the conscious realm. The night, however, is the custodian of the moon, the unconscious, and being a vital aspect of the feminine world, has historically been associated with the Virgin Mary. As we will see later, the moon has a very special relationship to the Madonna in her black aspect.

The emphasis on the night suggests that it is now the unconscious side of life—that which is far from conscious control—that will provide the message. And, indeed, this is the case in the response of Conrad. He had no control over it; nor, by the same token, did the pilgrims whose collective unconscious psyche this legend touched. In the midst of the dark, the light shone brighter than the sun. The light was centered around the altar of Mary itself. In the *Mysterium Coniunctionis*, Jung mentions that "Luna is really the mother of the sun, which means, psychologically, that the unconscious is pregnant with consciousness and gives birth to it. It is the night, which is older than the day. . ." and "from the darkness of the unconscious comes the light of illumination, the *albedo*. The opposites are contained in it *in potentia*. . ."[6] The "sun" (light and consciousness) was present on that legendary night in the form of the spontaneous luminescence of the altar, which had a glow "brighter than that of the sun at midday." Such a description is clearly archetypal, borrowed from the realm of the Divine itself. Further, it was around the Virgin Mother that this light shone, which in effect glorified her in particular. Sol (sun) and Luna (moon) were both present in the form of the Virgin Mary and the emanating light. The scene combines these two principles into a meaningful unity. Sun and moon are a part of a single vital process of life, each representing two different aspects of both nature and the human psyche. One could just as well use the terms Logos and Eros, Logos being equated with the masculine consciousness based on discrimination, judgment, and insight, while Eros with feminine consciousness and the capacity to relate.[7] As Jung puts it, again in the *Mysterium Coniunctionis*,

Logos and Eros are intellectually formulated intuitive equivalents of the archetypal images of *Sol* and *Luna*.[8]

That these two principles, which are a part of not only life in general but certainly of the human psyche, should come together in such a dramatic archetypal manner shows the importance of this Divine Dedication in the history of the monastery. The Virgin Mother was elevated from an insignificant position, or at the very most a respected one, onto an equal footing with the Godhead. Even at this early stage, the black aspect of the Madonna is foreshadowed, especially in this being a revelation of the night, as well as in the legend's unorthodox expression.

The Dedication was not a product of conscious intent, but rather of unconscious forces forever at play. It was an expression of the union of Logos and Eros, consciousness and unconsciousness, spirit and matter. According to Jung,

> The psychological union of opposites is an intuitive idea which covers the phenomenology of this process. It is not an "explanatory" hypothesis for something that, by definition, transcends our powers of conception. For, when we say that conscious and unconscious unite, we are saying in effect that this process is inconceivable. The unconscious is unconscious and therefore can neither be grasped nor conceived. The union of opposites is a transconscious process and, in principle, not amenable to scientific explanation.[9]

In the same way, the Virgin Mother in her blackness and the legend of the Divine Dedication can never be understood in theological or psychological terms alone. Psychology is but one significant light among many others that can greatly enhance one's living relationship to what the legend signifies, and that can show how, even at this early time, the way was being paved for the appearance of the Black Madonna.

The details of the legend are in themselves quite unique. Conrad's vision of Jesus before the altar—of His mother as High Priestess—is an act of veneration of the highest degree. The Ris-

en Lord sacrifices on the altar dedicated to His mother. Again,
theologically, the patriarchal trinitarian godhead recognizes and
sanctifies the place of the Lord's mother. She is life, that which
gives birth, nourishes and in the end takes back again. In the
vision, it is Jesus who can stand before her – he who has himself
been torn between life and death, and stretched between every
possible ambiguity that life offers – and who in the end offers himself to her. It is he who has the chance for a psychic-spiritual renewal. To stand victorious before her and offer a sacrifice at her altar
is to affirm life with a level of wisdom that knows, paradoxically,
that the very sufferings and torments which one would be gladly
rid of, are, in fact, the means of transformation to a higher nature.

That Jesus is accompanied by the four evangelists suggests a
sense of wholeness, but a wholeness that is grounded in its relationship to this feminine principle. Reflections of wholeness are
quite different from a relationship to or experience of it. Conrad's vision seems to point out that there was a very special and
undoubtedly unique value and *whole*-someness related to this Virgin Mother and still lurking in the collective unconscious, but
only just then beginning to emerge.

The unorthodox nature of the legend is also seen in the alterations which St. Conrad made in the *Sanctus, Benedictus,* and *Agnus Dei* in his *De secretis secretorum* (see pages 25-26).

In Conrad's *Sanctus,* the line "*Sanctus Deus in aula gloriosae Virginis, miserere nobis*" (Holy God in the realm of the Glorious Virgin, have mercy upon us) changes the emphasis from the "Lord
God of Sabaoth" alone to his relationship to the Virgin Mother.
He is now seen "*in aula gloriosae Virginis,*" that is, in the realm of
the glorious Virgin. From this setting he is asked to have mercy.
Such a change seems to suggest that his judgments of and relatedness to mankind must now be measured against the feminine
principle as embodied by the Virgin. God as a father alone is not
desired. Rather, *De secretis secretorum* says that the feminine ought
to be considered as a vital reality in God's relationship to humanity.
The psyche needs more than just a patriarchal standpoint and

perspective on the world. It also needs the feminine, that is, the willingness to accept and be involved in the vital irrational processes of life that are not immediately amenable to conscious judgments and explanations.

The *Benedictus* also shows this relationship to Mary: *Benedictus Mariae filius in aeternum regnaturus, qui venit in nomine domini.* (Blessed is the Son of Mary reigning in eternity, who comes in the name of the Lord). As they were shouted by the people to Jesus as he entered Jerusalem (John 12:13), the words refer to Jesus as the son of Mary. Jesus must be seen also as the Son of a Mother, not just as Son of a Father. To know the fullness of life, one must recognize one's heritage from both principles. In the same way, Conrad's *Agnus Dei* is a prayer for both the living and the dead, which is to say that the dynamic force behind what we call "God" ought to relate to not only our present conscious orientation, but also to the world beyond concrete experience — to the realm beyond consciousness: *Agnus Dei, qui tollis peccata mundi, miserere vivorum in te pie credentium, miserere mortuorum in te pie quiescentium, da pacem vivis et defunctis in te pie regnantibus* (Lamb of God who takes away the sins of the world, have mercy upon the living who believe in you piously, have mercy upon the dead who are resting in you piously, give peace to the living and the dead who are reigning in you piously). Here is an appeal for God to touch our total psyche, not only our psyche *per se*, but that which is about us in tangible form and that which is behind and ahead of us in history and not so easily grasped. The archetypal nature of the psyche is rooted in the past, but also extends into the future. That which is behind us must be blessed and that which is before us must be accepted in order that the psychic-spiritual nature of man in all its fullness may move forward into the future.

Such alterations reflect the need to have a place for the feminine and to make room for the irrational, *i.e.*, that which is beyond our present understanding. These are unorthodox alterations only in context of a strictly patriarchal religion. In themselves, however, they help to restore the balance so badly needed in the Western understanding of God. This is especially so when these alterations are set and maintained within the framework of the legend itself.

When such unorthodox phenomena do not appear in the context of a legend but erupt spontaneously in the life of an individual, the effect can be extremely powerful. My German analysand, Anna, experienced the following three dreams over a six-month period:

> (March) I see the Black Mother at a table, lighting two candles. The Holy Day has come. She puts them in the middle of the table where they shine in darkness. She blesses the cup of wine laced with fire and gives it to all her children that wait for her around the table. Then she feeds them the bread and feeds them with herself. This is the Mass.

> (August) I saw the Black Madonna in a dream. She was sitting at a table with many people. The scene was like Jesus at the Last Supper. She was very black and also wore a black garment, the end of which she had put over her head as a veil. The garment had a wide orange-yellow border. Her dark face had an unearthly beauty; it radiated transcendence. She looked at me, and I liked it.

> (October) I dreamed I measured Catholic liturgical vestments in order to sew new vestments myself. But the one I was making was meant to be worn by women in the service of the Black Madonna. Therefore I made my vestment 70 cm longer than the traditional ones so that its proportions would be elegant and the lines flowing. The color had to be green and the fabric pure silk. The material and everything connected with it had to come from an unspoiled, natural source. I planned to add precious embroidery like it had never been done before. The priestess of the Black Madonna would wear it while saying Mass in honor of God the Mother. Then I discovered that hair grew out of my fingertips. I thought this strange but accepted it. The same thing happened to my sister. The hair made our hands very sensitive.

These three dreams clearly place the feminine in a central position in the spiritual development of this woman. It must be remembered that she came from a patriarchal family and culture, a setting that gave little value to the feeling functions of life and relationships. There are archetypal dimensions in these dreams which represented, for this woman, a long-awaited healing power. The integration of the feminine and its dark side unleashed a wave of creativity and made it possible for her to once again accept her Germanic ancestry in a renewed way. The hair growing from her fingertips is a direct reference to this creative potency which reflected itself ever so powerfully in her paintings. Fortunately this woman was able to accept the unorthodox nature of these dreams, indeed she even welcomed it. It was as though her patriarchal experience had become so extreme that any movement of the pendulum in the opposite direction was a welcome improvement.

In the legend surrounding the consecration of the Chapel, it was before Mary's altar that the Mass was celebrated by her own Son. The title of Conrad's book, *De secretis secretorum*, is most appropriate, for that which cannot be formulated in the precision of dogma moves over into the realm of mystery. An insight into the mystery of life becomes a cherished secret in many mystery religions; such mysteries are not easily grasped nor readily dispensed.

Of course it can be asked just why such a place as the Holy Chapel of Einsiedeln could have been blessed with such a visitation and Divine Dedication. Certainly the psychic groundwork must have been well prepared for such a legend to express itself so well and so suddenly in the collective consciousness. Not only does the legend show that the times were right for its expression, it also demonstrates that something vital was going on in the collective psyche. It seems to point out that there was a living relationship with the Madonna in her dark aspect—as seen in her association with the night, as well as her unorthodox appearance. The darkness is a living part of the archetype, and in this legend it comes through in a positive and unifying way.

Though over-speculation here is risky, it would seem that such a legend was possible because of the Madonna's venerated position in the monastery. The monastery was under her protection;

the life of the community spiritually and architecturally revolved about her. Not so easy to answer but interesting to ask is whether there was something special about this particular Virgin Mother that distinguished her from other centers dedicated to Mary. What was the force behind her that could create such a powerful legend? Veneration of Mary was nothing new at this time, but to such a degree was certainly unique.

Though this may not be the sole factor, her setting in the Finsterwald seems to have undoubtedly played an important role. It was not the usual locale nor a traditional center for a religious development of the Virgin Mother. It was unknown territory, the dark and somber area that was a direct antithesis to all things cultural and civilized at the time. For St. Conrad and the pilgrims, to find the Virgin Mother there, and so nobly venerated against the background of the Finsterwald, may well have been the psychic catalyst for such a revelatory legend. It could also be reversed somewhat to say that because the Virgin was in the Finsterwald, she was accordingly venerated in so special a manner. Because the light and dark of wholeness were able to exist side by side in mutual respect, the vision became all the more an expression of that very psychic wholeness. It was an expression of the unconscious encouraged by a unique natural setting which had the effect of balancing the light and the dark sides of life. The dark unconscious background always stood just minutes from the Lady Chapel. Psychologically, the unconscious needs a means of expressing itself, and once it finds one, it will reveal itself with increasing import relative to one's respect for and involvement in the revelations it provides. Set against the background of the Finsterwald, the Virgin Mother may well have elevated that unconscious message to a degree of importance and value not often attained. Such a divine assembly and consequent Dedication should be considered a foreshadowing of the uniqueness of the Virgin Mother of Einsiedeln—a uniqueness that only a few centuries later blossomed forth and revealed itself in the phenomenon of the Black Madonna.

The monastery that Eberhard built burned down in 1029,
though it is said that the chapel housing the Virgin Mother was
unharmed. In 1031, Embrich, the fifth Prince Abbot, laid the foundation stone of another church and monastery, which was completed in 1039. This was an important date because the remains
of St. Meinrad were brought back from Reichenau for the consecration of the new structure on October 13. This again underscores the relationship between the Virgin Mother and the first
hermit, Meinrad, a factor that will be mentioned in more detail
later.

A second fire struck on May 5, 1226. This fire was not so severe, and the church was rebuilt the same year. Again it is said
that the Holy Chapel was untouched. Conrad I, Count of Thun,
then the reigning Prince Abbot, undertook the building of the
third monastery, which survived for 239 years. In 1465 the church
was again destroyed by fire. Though a great deal was lost, the Holy
Chapel was reportedly untouched. In actuality, however, the fire
started in the Holy Chapel, and it is more than likely the building and the then-existing statue of the Virgin Mother were destroyed. It was after this fire that a reconstruction of the Chapel
of the Virgin Mother was undertaken. Though this was completed,
the extension to the monastery which was included in the same
plan was never completed, due to a fourth fire on March 30, 1509.
The damage was not severe, and according to tradition the chapel again was completely untouched. Sixty-eight years later, in 1577,
the final and perhaps the worst fire struck. It lasted just a few
hours, but the entire village of Einsiedeln plus the monastery and
church were destroyed.[10] Though the roof and towers of the
church were destroyed, the main destruction was external, with
little interior damage. Again, the Holy Chapel was said to have
been unharmed. The fifth monastery was rebuilt in the same style
and shape as the previous one, although the construction was
very poor. In 1721 Abbot Schenklin of Wyl laid the foundation
stone of the present Church, which was consecrated in 1735.

Thus from the time of Meinrad's death in 861 until 1577, a period of 716 years, the monastery suffered five different fires. After each fire, the buildings were rebuilt, and each time the Holy Chapel was centrally positioned. After each fire, the chapel was left untouched, at least according to tradition. To the people of the village it must have signified there was something special about that structure and its Virgin Mother.

During the fire of 1509, Abbot Conrad went into the Chapel to pray to the Mother of God. He said, "Oh, Mary, Mother of God, take heed, for all that is here is thine and belongs wholly to thee." He proclaimed afterward that the fire would not come near the Abbot's house which, in fact, was the case." One can be sure that not only Abbot Conrad but the people as well were confident of the miraculous survival of the Chapel, and in its ability to renew itself through each reconstruction. The five fires over this span of time are certainly a crude reminder of the capricious nature of life, of those unexpected unknowns in life that take as easily as they give. There was a high degree of unpredictability in the monastery's history, an unpredictability and capriciousness that is not only consistent with the psychological aspects of the Black Madonna, but might even be directly though unwittingly attributable to her. This can be seen in Abbot Conrad's prayer during the fire of 1509. He addressed his prayer to her, acknowledging that she had control over the fire, and by logical deduction concluding that she could direct its beginning and end.

All prayers to a god or goddess seek supplication from them as the controllers and causes behind particular dangers and predicaments. Such prayers reflect the psychological acceptance of a reality that is only dimly perceived at the conscious level. At deeper levels of the psyche, the notion of God is easier to understand and accept than it is theologically. God is psychologically comparable to the Self, and in a certain sense the two concepts are interchangeable. As Jung puts it,

> Their [mandalas] object is the *self* in contradistinction to the *ego*, which is only the point of reference for consciousness, whereas

the self comprises the totality of the psyche altogether, *i.e.*, conscious *and* unconscious. It is therefore not unusual for individual mandalas to display a division into a light and a dark half, together with their typical symbols... It is at the same time an image of God and is designated as such... Correspondingly, in the Western mandala, the *scintilla*, or soul-spark, the innermost divine essence of man, is characterized by symbols which can just as well express a God-image, namely the image of Deity unfolding in the world, in nature, and in man.[12]

The Black Madonna is the religious expression of one facet of the Godhead, and is also a vital extension of the Self with its dark, unconscious, mysterious, unpredictable nature. Theologically, it is very difficult to accept that God has both a light and dark side, that He carries both masculine and feminine energies, and that He is the director of both creative and destructive forces. Such a view clashes head-on with Judeo-Christian theology. Yet psychologically, such a view is a partially recognized admission of the dual nature of the psyche, namely, not only that which gives but also that which takes, not only the known but also the unknown, not just what is under our conscious control but also what comes from other areas of the psyche.

One could ask if in fact the Black Madonna does not more easily carry the projections of the capricious nature of the Godhead than does "God the Father." The dark side of the Father is seen in judgments and can be, in theory, traceable to logical causes, but the dark side of the Mother is illogical, irrational, unwarranted and apparently meaningless. This is the side that is hard to integrate, for the unconscious always interferes through psychic "burnings" and "devastations," which so quickly undo the hard-earned accomplishments of our conscious efforts. We call it misfortune, hard luck, or even evil; but to recognize that such happenings may themselves be a necessary part of psychic-spiritual growth and maturity is the new task for people today.

Though the fires represent only a portion of the hardship the monastery faced over the centuries, their frequency and impact is impressive, so much so that they could be compared, on a larger scale, to the transformative fires of Medieval alchemists. For the latter, fire was often the *prima materia* from which a more refined product emerges.[13] It was also a part of the *incineratio*, the burning and bringing to ashes before change can take place. The monastery fires did not signify destruction, but rather a means to renewal and further development. The integration of that hard truth is a vital step toward a wisdom so beautifully projected in the Black Madonna. Popular opinion has it that she herself became black due to fire-damage.[14] We will see that this is in fact not the case; however, she is associated with fire, if for no other reason than the legend that her chapel survived five of them. Yet behind the prayer of Abbot Conrad lies a probable truth—that she not only protects from fires, but also instigates them. In other words, she represents that psychic force which not only sustains but also destroys and brings to life again.

History ascribes the blackening of the Einsiedeln Black Madonna to an entirely different factor, one which also highlights a collective desire to keep the Madonna black. Though sources vary as to the actual age of the present Black Madonna, it is certain that the original color was not black, but rather the flesh tones of a typical European.[15] Over the course of the centuries, however, the natural white flesh color became blackened by the large votive candles that stood by her. The number of these candles varied from time to time as each Canton gave a candle in her honor. One source says that there were five silver lamps that used to burn night and day before the statue, and, in front of her altar, there were formerly sixteen large tapers which were kept constantly burning. These tapers weighed from twenty to thirty kilograms each, and produced not only light but fumes as well.[16] The interesting feature is that as the Madonna became black, the people forgot that she was originally of a white flesh color. Black became the color associated with her, a color with which the collective was more than just passingly content.

The presence of so many candles itself is impressive. One would have to use one's imagination to picture what it would have been like in the days before electricity. Without candles, the chapel, which was inside yet another building, would be extremely dark. With the candles, it became possible to see the Madonna and to glorify her. Fire, as mentioned above, symbolizes psychic energy. The mysterious substance of life itself is offered to her through fire. With this light, one was able to take her into consciousness—in effect, to redeem her, as the alchemists say, from the "black blacker than black," the uncomprehensible darkness. For the unconscious in its crude undifferentiated state to develop, energy must be applied, work must be performed, an offering must be made.

The "real" color of the Einsiedeln Madonna did not become known again until after the French invasion of May, 1798.[17] When the French came, they took what they thought was the original statue and sent it off to Paris. In fact, however, they took a duplicate that had been moved into the sanctum from the hospital chapel just a few days before the invasion. The original was placed in a chest and was brought on May 2, 1798, to the neighboring Alpthal, and soon after that up the Haggenegg above Schwyz. A chapel now stands where it was hidden. It was soon realized that this was not a terribly good hiding place, and so the Stifts steward, Placidus Kalin, pretending to be a peddler, carried it on his back over the Rhine to the Kloster of St. Peter in Bludenz, Vorarlberg, in Austria. This is a considerable distance by foot, which accordingly reflects the tremendous popular faith in and closeness to the Black Madonna. The statue remained there until March 23, 1799, when it was taken to the Provost office of St. Gerald. There the chest was opened, and it was immediately decided that a renovation was needed. During this renovation, it was discovered that the original statue was not black—a fact long since forgotten.[18]

It is interesting to speculate that the Black Madonna embodied Einsiedeln, so that to possess her would be, symbolically, to possess the entire community as well. In this regard, it should be mentioned that in 1018 the monastery received from Emperor Henry II a charter constituting the Abbot as sovereign ruler of the valleys of the Sihl and Alp, a total of about 45,000 acres. Though it is true that in 1434 the Canton of Schwyz took the title of "*Schirmvogt mit dem Recht der hohen Gerichtsbarkeit*" (Protector with the right of seigniory), the Abbot still nominally remained the sovereign ruler.[19] This lasted until 1798, the time of the French invasion. The point here is that political sovereignty resided at Einsiedeln. Thus, to the French, to take the statue of the Virgin Mother would be tantamount to taking the entire canton. They were *her* lands and reflected the extent of her power. She was thus a sort of regional soul-image; psychologically, she was one significant collective expression of the collective unconscious.

According to the written account of the restoration, popular outcry demanded that the Virgin Mother remain entirely black. The account states that not even the eyes, nor cheeks, nor lips should be a different color, and this demand was acceded to by the reverend fathers.

It would seem that, at least by this time, the projections of the dark aspects of the psyche had transferred themselves from the Finsterwald to the Black Madonna. The several preceding centuries did have a refining function. As the Virgin Mother took on more blackness, the less the same projections were placed on the Finsterwald. As the centuries passed and a sense of civilization moved into Einsiedeln, the surrounding woods became correspondingly less dark and gloomy. It might even be suggested that the less dark the Finsterwald, the more black the Madonna became. The darkness of the feminine world, like any aspect of an archetype, does not simply disappear; when it ceases to be associated with one particular element, one can be sure it will seek to express itself elsewhere. By the time of her renovation, the Madonna was no crude representation of the dark side of life and the psyche, but was instead highly refined and fully glorified in the collective heart and mind—not just as a run-of-the-mill Virgin Mother, but as the Black Madonna of Einsiedeln.

Chapter Two—Notes

[1]Ida Luethold-Minder, *Madonna im Finstern Wald*, p. 18

[2]*Einsiedeln "In the Dark Wood,"* p. 35

[3]*Ibid.*, p. 38

[4]*Ibid.*, pp. 22-25

[5]*Ibid.*, p. 38

[6]C.G. Jung, *CW* XIV, p. 177

[7]*Ibid.*, p. 179

[8]*Ibid.*, p. 180

[9]*Ibid.*, p. 381

[10]"Brief Guide to the Abbey of Our Lady of the Hermits, " p. 6

[11]*Einsiedeln "In the Dark Wood,"* p. 41

[12]C.G. Jung, *CW* IX, i, p. 389

[13]C.G. Jung, *CW* XII, pp. 232, 317

[14]von Franz, *Shadow and Evil in Fairytales*, p. 105

[15]The "Brief Guide to the Abbey of Our Lady of the Hermits" (p. 3) places the date after the fire of 1465. *Our Lady of Hermits* (p. 20) puts the completion of the statue at 1466, in time for the Angelic Dedication. *Einsiedeln "In the Dark Wood"* (p. 82) dates the statue to the ninth century.

[16]Einsiedeln "In the Dark Wood," p. 82

[17]The effect of this invasion is well documented in Ringholz, *Wallfahrtsgeschichte*, pp. 26-28

[18]The actual first-person account of the restoration is worth citing in full:

I the undersigned, Johann Adam Fuetscher, painter and court flag-bearer of the dominion of Blumenegg in Vorarlberg, a native of Ludesch, wish to make with this writing an avowal and public testimony. I do this in the absence of the most Reverend Holy Imperial Prince and Abbot of Einsiedeln as well as the Chapter and Holy Deacon, who are now at St. Gerald where they took refuge because of the French invasion of Switzerland. I have been called in order to inspect and make the necessary repairs of the miraculous image of the most blessed Divine Mother, which had been secretly stored away and accordingly saved. I found the miraculous wooden image in the following condition:

First, I noticed that it had been artfully carved. In antiquity it had been illuminated, showing distinguishable traces of gold flowers and golden borders. I also discovered obvious traces that the wooden image had been initially covered with a linen cloth to which the colors had stuck.

The face was thoroughly black. This color is not attributable to a painter but to the smoke of the lights of the hanging lamps which for so many centuries always burned in the Holy Chapel at Einsiedeln. It was very clear to me that the face had been initially entirely flesh colored, which is revealed by the fallen-off crust still in my keeping.

I found the child which was sitting on the left arm to be of the same color as the mother in both its face and its hair. As every evidence shows, the body of the child is also prepared in flesh color, which clearly proves that both the child and mother were painted a natural flesh color.

I found secondly that the holy miraculous image had been greatly damaged on the surface, especially in the area of the face. Here the material had actually fallen off up to the whitewashed priming in several places. In other places it had only partially fallen off. In still others it held fast. I must conclude therefore that the image must have been kept during its flight in a very moist and even wet hiding place. Hence, I undertook the following restoration:

After I removed all the waste and soluble material from the face, I then smoothed the solid color parts as much as possible. I then painted the entire face of both the mother and the child black as it previously had been. Further, I painted over the damaged belt as well as the lining of the dress on the sleeves and border. I painted them a simple blue, although as is clearly seen [the statue] to [its] lowermost border appears to have been gilded.

Finally, I went over the entire dress of the miraculous image with smoked oil and distilled linseed oil, which I hoped would better preserve it in the future.

The miraculous image had been carved with its eyes open. Since it was painted completely black, however, it seemed to be without eyes. Because of this someone advised me to at least distinguish the pupils with some blue and white and also to temper the black on the cheeks and lips with a little rouge. Having done this, I finished my work.

By itself, the change of the eyes and cheeks was just a little thing. It nevertheless contrasted just a little too much with the formerly completely black form. At the public display of the image at Bludenz, several persons who had seen it before at Einsiedeln in the Holy Chapel took occasion to express some doubts concerning the genuineness [Echtheit] of the miraculous image. They did this because it was no longer the same color. So after this rather solemn exposure, and at the request of the above-mentioned Lords of the Capital of Einsiedeln who were at St. Peter's in Bludenz, I covered again with black paint the entire face, including the eyes, of both the Mother and Child.

Maria, who has honored me to serve at this work with my unworthy hands, reach to me as a reward in my hour of death, and give me your powerful hand and lead me to your divine Son who has glorified this your image through so much wonder and grace.

To this most conscientious testimony and confirmation, I have signed this writing as an eternal document of truth with my own signature and set with my seal. This has been done at the Provost Office of St. Gerald, August 9, 1799, and again at St. Peter near Bludenz on September 9, 1799.

I, Johann Adam Fuetscher, ornamental painter, testify as set forth.

[19]*Our Lady of Hermits*, p. 1

3

THE DARK
IMAGE THAT TRANSFORMS

The present statue of the Virgin Mother of Einsiedeln probably came into being after the fire of 1465. The fire broke out
in the Chapel and destroyed all the woodwork, so the old statue
was undoubtedly destroyed and a new one needed. At the same
time, the monastery had to be rebuilt as quickly as possible. The
old statue was probably a seated figure, as many contemporary
woodcuts depict. The origins of both the old and new statues
are uncertain, though many theories about them have been
proposed.[1]

The earliest record of the possible origin of the present Madonna
dates to 1555, from the town clerk at Burgheim,[2] whose records
describe an interesting and humorous incident, which at the same
time reveals some insights concerning this question. The story
goes that during one of the pilgrimages at Einsiedeln, a group
of people gathered one evening in one of the local inns. The group
was discussing the various signs and wonders of the Virgin Mother,
referring constantly to her emanating love. There was a man there,
however, who was not a pilgrim but had come to Einsiedeln on
a business matter. After this man had listened for a while, he too

45

got up and talked about his relationship to the Virgin Mother:

> As she is esteemed so highly among you, so I must also say that she is my sister!

The pilgrims and the innkeeper were outraged at this talk. The news quickly spread to the Abbot, who promptly sent the man to the tower for the night. The next morning the man was brought before a council for further questioning. He answered:

> Yes, the Maria at Einsiedeln is my sister and what is still more— the Devil at Konstance and the Great God at Schaffhausen are my brothers!

The man was accused of blasphemy. The superior judge, however, questioned him further, believing there might have been something behind such a boast. To his questions the man replied:

> I have spoken justly, for my father was a sculptor and did make the Devil at Konstance and likewise the Great God at Schaffhausen and in like manner your Maria here in your Chapel of Grace— besides also me; therefore, we are all four brothers and sister!

The statue is late Gothic and appears to have originated in northern Switzerland or southern Germany. It is a wooden figure not quite four feet tall. The dress is a rust color with gold hems and a gold belt. The hair of both the Virgin and the Child is gold. The hands and face of the Mother and the entire body of the Child on her left arm, as well as the bird in his hand, are all painted black. She stands on a green base (see figure four).

The detailing of the statue is particularly interesting. The average visitor might not notice, for example, that the Child is holding a bird in his left hand. However, if he did see this, it would be very unlikely that he would also see that the bird is pecking at His thumb. There is also a beautiful gold casket at the feet of the Madonna. What the stranger would probably not know is that (until recently*) inside this casket lies the skull of St. Mein-

---

* (Ed. note) This skull, which has been removed and reconstructed, is now housed in a container behind the high altar.

rad, the founder of the Hermitage (see figure five). The Madonna's queenliness is emphasized by the wand or scepter she holds in her right hand, as well as by the gold crown on her head. The dynamism and power literally surrounding her is underscored by a dazzling array of gold clouds and lightning. Below her and on top of the casket stands a gold crucifix. In addition, both she and the child are clothed in elaborate garments, called hangings, which are changed according to various seasons of the church year. The monks sing her the *Salve Regina* (Hail Mary) daily.

A great deal more could be said about this statue, but one thing which is often taken for granted is the obvious relationship between Mother and Child—both are black. Theologically, a great deal can and has been said about this relationship, but in psychological terms this fact is crucial. It is not uncommon for goddesses of various kinds to be seen holding an infant boy in their arms or laps; the archetypal relationship between mother and son figures strongly in world religions. On the higher level of the feminine, the mother is not simply "mother," but the mother transformed in every respect. Her childbearing is no commonplace event, but rather the birthing of a divine child.' This is very clearly seen in the Madonna at Einsiedeln, which represents a highly refined transformative process away from the crudely maternal Finsterwald. The Madonna carries her son, her own creation. According to Erich Neumann,

> The woman gives birth to this divine son, this unconscious spiritual aspect of herself; she thrusts it out of herself not in order that she herself may become spirit or go the way of this spirit, but in order that she herself may be fructified by it, may receive it and let it grow within her, and then send it forth once more in a new birth, never totally transforming herself into it.'

In effect this means that the unconscious gives birth to consciousness without making any attempt or having any desire to identify itself with it. At the same time the unconscious can be worked and stimulated to new creative expression by the efforts of consciousness. Neither should be transformed into the other. The child is the expression of the spiritual nature of the feminine. Like the Kore in the Greek myth, the Madonna at Einsiedeln becomes a "bearer of light." As Neumann continues,

> Her luminous aspect, the fruit of her transformative process, becomes the luminous son, the divine spirit-son, spiritually conceived and spiritually born...[5]

In short, the Child is the aspect of the Mother that must necessarily express itself as the latter approaches the light. The light impregnates her and causes her to give birth to light. In other words, when the unconscious approaches consciousness, or when consciousness "impregnates" unconsciousness with its own spiritual nature, the result will be a "divine child," a new consciousness of a higher nature—higher because its parents are *both* aspects of the psyche (conscious and unconscious), and it reconciles the two. Jesus is well known as the Son of His Father, and is thus very much connected with Spirit. Here He is also the Son of his Mother and accordingly related to matter, to flesh and blood and to the affairs of everyday life. Both principles meet in him. In his *Aion*, Jung mentions that Christ is a symbol of the Self,[6] or the center of the psyche symbolizing psychic wholeness. If the same is true of the Mother and Child at Einsiedeln, it could be said that the center point of the psyche, the Self, is borne in the arms of the maternal side of the personality, namely the unconscious. Alchemy expresses this by saying that the *prima materia* is the mother of all things, and above all of the *lapis* (stone), the *filius philosophorum* (son of the philosophers).[7] The *lapis* is frequently equated with Christ. That the Child too is black seems almost to be a compensatory factor for commonplace emphasis on his light side. Again, it must be said that he is not only the son of the father/conscious/light side, but also of the mother/unconscious/dark side.

Unconsciousness spiritualizes itself in consciousness, that is, it finds a measure of liberation in creation from its own sources, without at all emptying itself or identifying with consciousness. For one who is reasonably conscious, this means an acceptance of that dark life-giving force in one's own psyche. To be the child of light alone is too easy and simplistic; the ego becomes cut off from its life-giving source. Such an attitude translated into every-day life leads one down a path of sentimentality and naiveté. However, to be a child of the darkness as well, where the light is not so bright and the answers (or even questions) are not so clear, brings one fully into one's whole nature as a human being. Neumann continues:

> The study of depth psychology has shown that consciousness with its acquisitions is a late "son" of the unconscious, and that the development of mankind in general and of the human personality in particular has always been and must be dependent on the spiritual forces dormant in the subconscious.[8]

Without such a dependence, life is indeed one-sided.

There is also an interesting third figure to be considered. In his left hand, the Divine Child holds a small bird which is pecking his thumb. This bird is more that just a reference to the apocryphal legend that Jesus made little birds out of clay during his play time.[9] Though this seemingly strange gesture appears on the surface to be nonsensical, it plays an important part in the entire grouping.[10]

Some light might be shed here if we simply look at some of the ways in which the thumb has traditionally been viewed. The thumb is important in religion, for example in baptism, where it is used to make the sign of the cross, thus following the Old Testament custom of using the thumb to apply blood in ritual ordination.[11] In addition, the thumb and the first finger makes a circle, which with the other three fingers extended is often used as a blessing in the Greek Orthodox Church. The Moslem uses this same gesture while he recites his creed. The thumb and two fingers pointing upwards refers to the trinity. Even more apropos is the reference from the *Shvetashvatar Upanishad:*

A mighty Lord is Purusha...That Person, no bigger than a thumb, the inner Self, seated forever in the heart of man, is revealed by the heart, the thought, the mind. They who know That, become immortal.[12]

In the *Katha Upanishad*, we find:

That Person in the heart, no bigger than a thumb, burning like flames without smoke, maker of past and future, the same today and tomorrow, that is the Self.[13]

Here the thumb represents the very essence of man and, indeed, the cosmic order. In palmistry, the thumb is called "The Mount of Venus" and is associated with love, instincts, vitality, sensuality, fecundity, and bounty.[14] The thumb has also figured in Grimm's fairy tales, for instance "Tom Thumb" and the tale of "The Young Giant," where a child belonging to a farmer grows no larger than a thumb until he is taken away by a giant and suckled and cared for by him.

A very interesting reference to the thumb is found in the legendary Irish hero-warrior named Finn, who possessed the gift of magic prophetic powers. The legends differ as to how he got these powers, but they all agree that the warrior-hero-magician became possessed of second sight when he chewed his thumb, which had been burnt when immersed in a magic potion.[15] This wounded thumb motif appears in the Einsiedeln figure, in that the bird seems to be pecking at the Child's thumb. Whatever else can be said of the thumb, it is evident that it represents the very essence of man and his creative principle. According to Jung,

We know that Tom Thumb, dactyls, and Cabiri have a phallic aspect, and this is understandable enough, because they are personifications of creative forces, of which the phallus, too, is a symbol. It represents the libido, or psychic energy in its creative aspect.[16]

That a bird would peck the thumb seems to be a strong reference to the awakening of creative forces. This creative awakening is of a spiritual nature, for the simple reason that birds in general are symbolic of spiritualization (see Chapter One). As symbols of a higher power, they are often associated with gods and goddesses. Aphrodite has the dove and sparrow and Athena the owl. Accordingly, the Black Madonna of Einsiedeln also is associated with a bird, which in this case seems to be the very essence of the spiritual side of the Virgin Mother. As the Child is an expression of the Virgin Mother, and as consciousness is an expression of unconscious forces, the bird, the supreme spiritual principle, pecks at and thus quickens or enlivens the new consciousness at its creative center (the association of St. Meinrad with blackbirds, the ravens, should of course not be forgotten). As the mother of the new conscious outlook is the dark night of the unconscious, so too the creative urge in man is rooted in this same Black Mother. She is both the source of a new consciousness and the wellspring of all creativity. This bird is hers in that it "represents the stirrings or intuitions of the unconscious, the helpful mother."[17]

An interesting parallel to this is seen in two dreams of a forty-seven year old Protestant clergyman who consciously verbalized his own struggle with his lost creative side. For a number of years he had been the pastor of a very affluent congregation. Externally his world could not look much better. Internally, he was growing increasingly depressed and weary, and found less and less meaning in his work. Without any further call, he resigned his parish and started searching again for who he was. He dreamed that he was on the back of a bus and was feeling weary and dejected. The back door of the bus had a window which opened to about half the height of the door. He placed his hands through the open window and rested them on a rail "much as an expended athlete would." He continues:

> Suddenly, as I hung there lost in my thoughts, I had a terrible pain in the tips of my fingers. I looked up to see a train passing by (the heavy, iron wheels at least), and realized that the rail I had been resting my hands upon was a railroad track! I snatched

my hands back, horrified to even think that my fingers had been severed. They had not.

The dream goes on to say that at first the fingers did not bleed much, but then began to do so profusely. In the end the dreamer fears that the hospital will have to pull his nails out. With this he wakes up. The agony of his own creative side is dramatically represented, as is the shock his unconscious gave him. The bus with its collective overtones, his weariness and dejection at the age of forty-seven, and his own unconscious creative urges, are all represented. The wounding motif is clear enough, and yet what is a potentially severe wounding with a corresponding loss of life-blood can also be seen as an awakening to fuller consciousness. As the bird at Einsiedeln pecks the thumb of the Child and thus enlivens a new consciousness at its creative center, so a modern wounding (and a more severe one) has taken place in this dream, and ultimately for the same reason.

Five months later, the same man had a dream in which a black woman in her fifties or sixties instructed him on how to revive a dead bird. He was to rub the bird with his two fingers (index and middle) along its backbone just "along the spot where you would dig to get good meat to eat." He held the bird in his left hand. As soon as he did what was instructed, there were immediately two birds, very much alive. They both sat on fingers of his two hands.

> They both gently mouthed my fingers at first with their beaks, but . . . they became more and more excited — screeching and pecking my fingers more and more fiercely. It didn't hurt, but their frenzy startled me and I woke up slightly alarmed.

Again the creative side of his unconscious comes to him, but in a more gentle manner. The black woman, the resurrection of the bird, the possibility of eating the "good meat," and the pecking at his fingers, all obviously have their parallels with the grouping at Einsiedeln. They thus signal the awakening of the creative side of his unconscious. During these months, this man began and

completed a publishable manuscript as one means of giving vent
to these creative forces. He also gave serious consideration to how
he would return to a ministry in the church, but this time with
a renewed and restored connection to the creative ground of his
call.

Another man, thirty-two years old, dreamed that

> I am fishing inside a boathouse. I take much care to bait a hook
> with a worm. The worms are all taken out of a box and washed
> and lined up in a row. I select one and put it on a treble hook
> and attach the rest of the equipment. I think how unlikely it is
> that I will ever catch a fish like this because the treble hook would
> be much too large for any bait fish to bite one. I put the line in
> the water nonetheless, and instantly the bobber goes way under
> the water. I think I have a snag, curse, and start to pull in the
> line. I soon realize it is a fish and pull in a nice crappie. I tell my
> wife who is with me that I could catch a good mess of crappie
> for dinner if we are over a school. I go to take the hook out of
> the fish's mouth and grab it firmly behind the gills so it won't get
> free or bite or sting. Suddenly the fish grows to enormous size
> and struggles to get free. I have a firm hold and refuse to let it
> loose. It starts to chew on my fingers but I feel no pain and am
> unconcerned about harm as I still hold on to it. My wife is amazed
> and perplexed that I don't simply let the fish go. I wake up well
> aware that I am going to hold the fish. The feeling following the
> dream is very pleasant. I feel like a young boy, fishing without a
> care in the world on a lazy summer afternoon. I know I cannot
> return to that feeling all the time, though I would if I could. I
> wonder if I can have the feeling sometimes, though.

This man was a very conscious individual with a heightened degree of sensitivity and integrity. He was also a man who was in
a constant process of trying to integrate his dark and light sides.
He came from a background of open and sometimes violent de-
fiance of collective and particularly religious standards. When I
met him and at the time of this dream, he was happily married
with two children, working in a responsible position as a psy-
chotherapist and actively participating in a Christian congregation.

His dream pushed the whole issue of creativity and discovery to deeper levels. It is not uncommon for people to dream of fishing as a symbolic attempt to catch and bring up unconscious contents. The dream shows him being very deliberate about his bait and the use of a treble hook. He was indeed deliberate about how he looked within himself, but the use of the treble hook left him in doubt. This three-pronged hook recalls Neptune's trident. As God of the sea, he in turn is a contrast to earthbound life, that is, the conscious triune Christian God. Most people of Christian background who deliberately participate in the individuation process will at some time or another come to grips with the dark underworldly and not-so-orthodox side of what they know their God to be. These references to the "other side" of their God can often be as subtle as a dream of fishing with a treble hook. The fish that was caught was much larger than expected. The chewing of the fingers by the fish and the dreamer's struggle with it point again to this motif of creative awakening, and for this man perhaps, now with a previously unexperienced spiritual depth. This dream and the others mentioned are not uncommon, but consistently reflect the creative struggling of modern people and parallel the pecking of the thumb of the Christ child seen at Einsiedeln and similar places.

The Black Madonna's queenly authority and majesty is manifest in both the wand or scepter she carries in her right hand and the crown upon her head. The figure was apparently intended to hold a wand, which has often been attributed with magical properties. In this respect, it is not simply a symbol of authority, but more richly, a symbol of transformation commonly encountered in many fairy tales. According to the definition in *Man, Myth, and Magic*, the wand is

> also a means of aiming power at a given object; like the pointing finger or the pointing bone, it was once regarded as the agency of intense psychic power.[18]

The wand is a sign of wanderers, herdsmen, judges, leaders, priests and magicians. It is a special attribute of kings or their representatives.[19] The ancient physician-priests used the staff not only as a sign of authority but to also detect diseases; medieval physicians could be identified by the wands they carried. This fact is of some interest in that the Virgin Madonna at Einsiedeln is considered a healing goddess, as underscored by the many crutches and braces and devotional paintings of cured people hanging on the walls near her chapel.

The staff can be understood as a phallic symbol. As such it is a symbol of power and virility both supernatural and physical. According to Adolf Ammann,

> The staff means a guiding, directing, decisive principle, executive power, guidance, authoritative direction, straightness and consequence of the procedure, terms of reference, regulation, doctrine, canon, logos, guiding sense and destiny determining maturity. It points out the direction in which a spiritual attitude and conscious decision has to happen. In the hand of the Pope, of the governor and representative of Christ on earth, the staff gets the sign of absoluteness, of infallibility, of correct faith, of final judgment and of the final decision in the sense of the highest instance, which is shown with the confirming gesture equal to the judgment of God.[20]

It is a symbol of psychic energy.[21] To break the scepter is to sacrifice the particular direction of psychic energy to a specific task. It is a straight line and thus emphasizes this concept of direction as well as one's linear and sometimes obsessive concern for a given object.

That the Black Madonna would hold the staff in her right hand only seems to serve this idea more clearly. It must also be noted, however, that she holds in her right hand a necklace-like chain with a heart at the end of it. According to Cirlot's *Dictionary of Symbols*, "...the heart signifies love as the centre of illumination..."[22] Their being held in the same hand suggests that the scepter and heart are related, that is, that the Madonna rules in love and with a gesture of relationship and understanding that is not normally found in such abundance and flexibility in the collective standard. That they are both in the right hand emphasizes that it is her intent to govern in such a manner. This thus puts the Black Madonna in a position of authority and power, as well as making her a means of transformation, growth and healing.

The Black Madonna represents a life principle that can often defy collective standards. Psychologically, she is related to the unconscious. With the scepter in her hand, she represents, with her own ruling authority, the unconscious directedness that governs life. In this respect she is like Venus, in that Venus too was on the side of love and life. In fact there seems to be a hidden Venus quality to the Black Madonna which has a very definite allure. She represents that side of the psyche that leads and entices an individual into life in its fullest measure.

This Venus appeal will be mentioned in more depth later, but an interesting side of this relationship is borne out in figure six, where the Black Madonna is seen holding a very special scepter. This particular scepter strongly recalls the very popular folk song "Tannhäuser in the Venus Mountain," which is certainly not unknown in the part of Switzerland where the Black Madonna stands. In the song, Tannhäuser is told by the Pope that he will never be forgiven for living with Venus in the Mountain. The Pope says: "As on this dead staff in my hand, Never again a leaf shall grow, So from hell's all-consuming brand Salvation canst thou never know!" The story ends with this same Pope's staff breaking forth into leaves. There is a power greater than the Pope, who is the supreme spiritual head of the collective conscious order. It is such a scepter which the Madonna holds in her hand. It is not impossible that this very scepter, with the two leaves at the end, is directly related to the Tannhäuser myth. The Madonna carries that scepter of life and rules with an authority greater than any conscious comprehension, either individual or collective."[23]

The more passive aspect of her authority is her crown. On the one hand the crown is related to the sun (consciousness), being

in many cases a solar attribute, yet on the other it is related to
the mother (unconscious) because of its roundness. The idea of
roundness is inherent in the crown. As Jung expresses it in the
Mysterium Coniunctionis:

> This peculiar relationship between rotundity and the mother is
> explained by the fact that the mother, the unconscious, is the place
> where the symbol of wholeness appears.[24]

The crown is the symbol of preeminence, triumph and authority, which is why kings and gods wear them. This preeminence
lies especially in the fact that the crown not only sits upon the
top of the body, but also rises above it. Thus we speak of one's
"crowning achievements." This is more meaningfully seen in Christianity, where it is said that those who have conquered win the
"crown of eternal life." The alchemists spoke of the *corona* or *di-
adema cordis tui* (diadem of thy heart), by which they meant a
symbol of perfection. It thus becomes the crowning point of de-
velopmental process.[25] Here again the crown is also related to
the heart, which is not inconsistent with the heart-shaped form
that hangs from the Black Madonna's right hand. Her rule and
sovereignty is of the heart, of feelings, relatedness to the world
order, and inconsistency in human relationships not found in the
letter of the law. To recognize her crown is like recognizing the
authority and preeminence of the unconscious. It is to say that
psychic-spiritual wholeness is not possible without including the
unconscious in whatever form it may manifest itself.

The motif of the crown is extended to include the dramatic display of gold clouds and lightning that surrounds the Black Madonna. The lightning in particular has long been associated with her.
Woodcut prints dating back many centuries seem to make a point
of including this feature (see figure seven). The entire display
glorifies the Black Virgin. She is elevated to a celestial-spiritual
and dynamic position, the clouds emphasizing the former and
the lightning the latter. Both have long figured as fertile, lifegiv-
ing forces. In this respect, Augustine compared the apostles to

a cloud because of the fertilizing nature of prophesies which, like clouds, come from a higher order.[26] It is also said that lightning has an illuminating, vivifying, fertilizing, transforming, and healing function.[27] Lightning, especially, is representative of energy and power; it symbolizes psychic energy in its most dynamic form.

That both the lightning and crown are carved of gold places a high value on this aspect of the Black Madonna. There is a value in the dynamism of life. Gold is incorruptible, it does not tarnish, and neither does the dynamic quality of life represented by the Black Madonna. When life is viewed as hard, irreversible, and meaningless from a more logical point of view, she symbolically shows that life can still go on, and beckons in the blackness of life to accept the irreversible, which then makes it possible for life energy to move on in a new channel, and often in a more unique way.

A further consideration on the magnificent display of gold is simply that it is a metal that originates in the earth. Very much like the products of alchemy, gold lies buried and hidden in the black earth, waiting to be discovered through patient, careful work. The alchemical work begins with the *prima materia*, the black, and often ends with the inner acquisition of spiritual meaning, symbolized by gold itself. Because of its color, gold is associated with the sun of consciousness and can be seen as a symbolic link between earth and heaven, spirit and matter. It can then stand for the reconciling symbol; spirit and matter are not separated, but beautifully and dynamically joined.

From another perspective, however, the gold lightning and clouds are just not a glorification of the Black Madonna; they are in fact eclipsed by her. Such a thought is not inconsistent with the nature of the Virgin Mother, who is often associated with the moon. Mary is called the "Moon of the Church."

The moving experience of witnessing an eclipse has profound psychological importance. On one hand, the moon can be seen against the night skies in all of its brilliance when it is full; but on the other hand, there is a reversal during a solar eclipse, when the full moon appears quite black as it over-shadows the brilliance of the sun. What the moon does to the sun comes from her own dark nature.[28] An alchemical treatise, the *Consilium coniugli*, speaks of the moon as the shadow of the sun, yet "his [*i.e.*, the sun's] eclipse is changed to usefulness and to a better nature, and one more perfect than the first."[29] The sun and moon come together in a symbolic marriage. At the same time, this relationship reveals their antithetical nature, for the moon blocks the brilliance of the sun. The masculine and feminine principles of life, Logos and Eros, meet in a dramatic embrace. The coming together of these two principles and the drama of their struggle gives birth to a third and new thing, a son who unites the differences in himself.[30] In the same alchemical writing we find:

> So also the moisture of the moon, when she receives his light, slays the sun, and at the birth of the child of the Philosophers she dies likewise, and at the death the two parents are the food of the son[31]

The moon slays the sun, that is, she blackens it. In the end they both give way to the new product of their union, which in some ways may be likened to the feeling experience of a new dawn and the revitalization of nature after an actual solar eclipse.

The experience of revitalization from such an event is metaphoric of a new perspective and understanding of life, a consciousness new and vital simply because it draws its parentage from both the masculine and feminine dimensions, and thus brings about wholeness. The dawn of a new consciousness must come from the mutual involvement of the dark regions of the unconscious and the existing conscious outlook of an individual. As "parents," both are "food of the son." Both must struggle together before a new "Son" is born from them—a consciousness that unites both parents and resolves their conflict.

The way to this new consciousness is through an eclipse, that is, through the darkening of consciousness—classically expressed as a depression or introversion shrouded by doubt, feelings of hopelessness, fear, lack of meaning, and a sense that life is being threatened with stagnation and death. These are the same feelings a primitive might have had in watching an actual eclipse. Though modern man has gained some understanding of this natural process, he is still left with the same inner experience which grips him as firmly within his psyche as it would any unenlightened primitive. Unconsciousness threatens consciousness, but from the conflict that then ensues comes the possibility of a new insight, a higher wisdom, a renewal of life in its fullest sense.

In its own way the spectacle at Einsiedeln captures this psychic-spiritual experience. In her left arm, the Madonna holds the Child, the reconciling third thing. He is the new consciousness of mankind, yet he must go the way of his mother as well as of his father. In other words, he is born not only a child of the collective standards of his time, which for him and our own time have long been patriarchal; he is not just the child of the heritage of the collective with its consciously formulated insights, world views, and religious statements as rich as they may be; he is also the child of the dark uncertain side of life. His mother is the uncanny, ambiguous, indecisive yet fascinating side of the psyche that comes with a wisdom of its own and shakes the individual into a clear understanding that there is more to life than what is immediately apparent. Psychic-spiritual growth will come primarily from her and what she embodies. The Black Madonna of Einsiedeln is a collective expression in image form which compensates the collective conscious mentality of our age. In other words, for renewal to come in our time, it must be borne in the arms of the black, unknown maternal night of the unconscious, where humanity will once again open its psyche to that rich natural soil that is the mother of all human thought, invention, doctrinal formulation and truth. This new Son, Christ, has a dark side because of his association with his mother. This, too, obviously compensates the one-sided lightness of Christ too often emphasized in our culture.

Whether a viewer chooses to see the display of gold surrounding the Black Madonna as a glorification *of* or as an eclipse *by* the Madonna is not a matter of one view over another, since the two are not mutually exclusive. Any glorification of the dark principle entails a lessening of the light, and vice-versa. Any time a person chooses or is forced to look at his dark unconscious side, his conscious light is diminished and the unconscious side is accentuated and valued. This is a psychic necessity if creative growth is to take place.

The Black Madonna's ability to draw on the resources of the unconscious is reflected in her relationship with the skull of St. Meinrad, which has traditionally lain at the foot of the statue. The ancestors are a part of the unconscious from which we grow and in which our roots are planted. The soul had its seat in the head according to the ancient view; this soul corresponds to the modern unconscious, just as breath and lungs long ago were identified with consciousness.[32]

The skull signifies both the germ of the beginning and the seat of the soul, or the center of life. Sometimes, too, it represented the epitome of evil. When sufficiently depotentiated, it can serve as a talisman against its own evil.[33] The symbolic importance of the head or skull is a very widespread phenomenon, from its role among the head-hunters, the Dayaks, Bontoks, and Formosans, to the Irish, Arab, Fijian, and Congo practices of drinking from the skull as a means of gaining strength and curative powers. In the Solomon Islands, the skull was preserved in a sanctuary, and usually enclosed in a wooden object fashioned in the form of a fish or a miniature hut. It was believed that the skull is full of *mana* (power), and that through it the help of spirits could be obtained, especially through offerings.[34]

The skull is important for the very obvious reason that it "survives" (*i.e.*, outlasts) the living being. It can be said that the reverence of the head or skull and the necessity for decapitation marked man's discovery of his own spiritual nature as it resided in the head.[35] Because it survives the body, the skull takes on significance as a receptacle for life and for thoughts. Perhaps it was for this reason that it became especially important for the Celtic peoples. The human head for them served as a symbol of their entire religious life; they too believed that in it lay the human soul, the essence of things and the very nature of divinity it- self.[36] Their custom was to decorate human skulls with gold and use them as libation-cups. The skull became a protective talis- man, in that they believed that putting a picture of a head on daily utensils and objects would be beneficial. Indeed, much Celtic art is nothing more than representations of heads.

The Christian Church too has revered the skull and singled it out among its many relics. It is often adored and considered to possess miraculous powers. The head of St. Marnar, preserved at Aberchudes, was ceremonially washed every Sunday and the water was carried to the sick and diseased, who were said to re- cover their health after contact with it.[37]

Though such curative powers of the skull are not so prominent in St. Meinrad's case, his skull still holds a very important place in the Einsiedeln Abbey and its liturgy. Because the skull is a major symbol in a host of religions and mythologies, the role of that of St. Meinrad should thus not be thought of as an isolated phenomenon, but rather as one manifestation of a practically universal psychological motif.

Every January 21 (the anniversary of Meinrad's death) a Ponti- fical High Mass is celebrated. Before Vespers, the skull of St. Mein- rad is involved in a blessing of the people. Because of this gesture, the worshipper is connected with the "spirit" emanating from the skull. The spirit of St. Meinrad is brought before the people, which in a very dramatic way reminds them again of the religious life that made the hermitage possible. Yet there is more that just that. The ritual underscores the very means of renewal experienced not only by St. Meinrad, but potentially by everyone. The skull is a conveyor of spirit and a means of conferring ancestral power on the people. Yet it also thrusts one into the future in that it is a symbol of transformation. In Sabaean alchemy, the skull serves as a vessel of transformation,[38] not the intellectual sort, but one which involves the whole man and implies the process of death and rebirth. This in fact is "the Spirit of St. Meinrad," for as pointed out earlier his life was a transformation involving both death and rebirth the moment he entered the Finsterwald. His skull is not only the conveyor of the archetypal material of the collective unconscious, the "ancestors," but also the vessel of transformation for the present, and provider of hope for the future. The skull is a sign of death, yet any transformation of any worth must reckon with death not only physically but psychologically and spiritually. Only when submitting to such a factor will the ancestral voices be able to speak in a fertilizing, healing, and beneficial manner. When the head in all of its negative overtones is faced, it then becomes an "opener of the way."[39] To understand what that means is to gain a wisdom of the processes of life and death not readily grasped and too often avoided.

The vastness of archetypal material associated with the skull may seem quite remote to most. Yet no one today is exempt from the power of such archetypal memories living in the unconscious. Such memory traces often spontaneously appear in dreams just as powerfully as they did to any of our ancestors. The analysand of German heritage whom we already met, for example, dreamed the following:

> I dreamed of a black madonna holding a skull in her hands and standing on a skull. And around her there were more skulls in the plants and vines that surrounded her.

Two days later she dreamed:

> A batch of food was being prepared for me by somebody unknown to me. In the person's hands was a dark ball or sphere, which turned into a skull. The skull was called "The Black Madonna." That unknown person chopped the skull up and mixed it into some food for me. I had to eat that food.

These dreams place the issues of life and death before this woman and call her eucharistically to partake of this food. That she was able to do this is beautifully reflected in a dream she had five months later:

> I dreamed that I saw a black figure in front of me. This person was completely wrapped in black, and the head was covered with an executioner's hood. There were no round openings for the eyes, but two tiny slits made from silk. The figure underneath this horrible costume was alive and laughed loudly. Someone said, "That is my mother." Then the woman pulled the black henchman's hood off her head and out came the most horrible skull with still some decomposed and moldy flesh clinging to it. The woman started to turn ever so slowly. It was a terrible sight. Then the face started to change into a living face. It came alive and finally transformed itself into the lovely face of a young woman. She smiled kindly. A voice said something like, "sixteen envelopes" (and meant sixteen disguises or veils).
>
> The woman took me by the hands and danced with me an elegant and lovely dance. She was wearing a long, black garment. I said to myself, "I will remain European, this is not part of my culture. I will keep my long blue skirt and walking shoes. I will remain faithful to my own cultural heritage."

The realization that "That is my mother" reflects the truth that the feminine archetype lives in us all, that the Yin principle is very much alive if indeed veiled in our culture. To become aware of such an archetypal power is to become aware of the light and dark side of life and death, as well as of the fact that such a power will not come in just one way or in the way we would like, but will come with "sixteen veils," that is, in a variety of contradictory forms, yet all a part of a differentiated whole.[40] For this woman, it was as though she needed to be made fully aware of the horrible realities of death before such realities could transform themselves into a dance of life. The end of the dream suggest a reconciliation with her German past, a past that at one time had brought her so much pain.

The skull's relationship to the Black Madonna involves Her in the process of transformation. She assumes not just the quality of a loving divine mother, but a relationship with death itself as

well. Not only her relationship to the skull but her location in
the Cathedral suggests this. She stands in her own chapel at the
west end of the building. She faces west, which is traditionally
the land of death. This is no accident, for it is a long-standing
custom that the chancel of a church must be on the eastern side
of the building, that is, in the direction of the rising sun. The
Black Madonna faces the direction where the sun sets or "dies."

The West is also associated with the feminine. This was especially evident among the Aztecs, who deemed it the "place of wom-
en."[41] It was the womb of the earth from where mankind came
into existence. At the same time, it was seen as "the archetypal
womb of death destroying what has been born"[42]; it was the
place of origin and the place of return. The West becomes a threat
to consciousness if the latter is not mindful of its source and seeks
to sever its connections with its primal roots. In many ways this
is inevitable, for consciousness must struggle to establish its autonomy. But the wisdom offered by the West or by the Lady of
the West is that life and death are inseparable aspects of one process. According to Erich Neumann,

> . . .only after the world is created, after light has been made, after
> the sun has started on its course and the antithetical principle
> of hostile powers has gone into effect. . .does the west become a
> place of death.[43]

The sun or hero dies in the West to be born again in the East.
In one way or another every person must pass through this experience. Not only does a higher wisdom demand it, but a more
encompassing meaning to life compels it. The Black Madonna
must be considered in this context, for she does carry—in her
blackness and association with the West—the concept of death,
but more so, of death transformed.[44] This distinction is important since the Black Madonna is not associated with death alone,
but also with life; she seems to say that each must be viewed and
kept in balance by the other. That her stance would be toward
the West seems to compensate for the Western Christian view of

death as the enemy rather than as the possibility of new life, and as a means of transformation to a higher wisdom and nature.

This theme of death and rebirth is to some degree evident in the structure of the Chapel in which the Black Madonna stands. To a great extent, this chapel approximates the structure and feeling tone of a cave (see figure eight). It is constructed of black marble provided in 1617 by the Archbishop of Salzburg, Mark Sittich von Hohenems. This detail may seem relatively unimportant when first considered. But we could ask why it was *black* marble. It is probable that this fitted the very nature of what the Black Madonna had come to represent. It would certainly add to the mystery associated with her; she was and is literally surrounded by blackness. This effect is lost today because of electric lighting, but on days when it is not used, when the only means of light are the candles placed in the chapel, the illusion of a dark cave is very pronounced. Again, it must not be forgotten that the chapel is really a building within a larger building, thus increasing the darkness and need for candles.

Though it is true that the association of the chapel with a cave is grounded less in fact than fantasy, such an association is consistent with what caves have universally meant throughout the world. Caves have been used for a host of reasons, including temporary shelters, hiding places, permanent dwellings, sanctuaries and tombs. They have been the locale of birth and burial. Caves are very often a symbol of the original land of the dead." The cave of Machpelah in the field of Ephron the Hittite was purchased by Abraham (Genesis 23:1-9) for the burial of his wife Sarah—it was in a cave too that Jesus was buried after being crucified. It was from this same cave that he rose from the dead three days later, pointing to the cave as not only the place of death but also of transformation and rebirth. This is seen also in the Mithraic mysteries where the cult-hero fights the bull. As a part of the ritual he takes the bull into a cave, where he kills it. From its death comes forth fruitfulness and the riches of the earth." In this respect the cave is like a secret cavity enclosing a person

for the sake of renewal.[47] On the individual level this parallels
the process of vital change and renewal. According to Jung,

> Anyone who gets into. . .the cave which everyone has in himself,
> or into the darkness that lies behind consciousness, will find him-
> self involved in an—at first—conscious process of transfor-
> mation.[48]

The Black Madonna stands in her cave-chapel, at her feet not
only the skull of Meinrad, but the cross, a most fitting symbol
of wholeness. The cross signifies that such wholeness must go the
way of suffering and death and rebirth. Consciousness, with all
its existing attitudes and prejudices, must repeatedly give way to
a deeper, fundamental truth of life which can only come from
beyond, that is, from beyond consciousness, from the very depths
of the unconscious itself. A person possesses his own cave, the
unconscious, from which the mysteries of life and death are revealed.

   Saints and hermits have often been associated with caves. The
anchorite or reclusive life is practiced by Buddhist hermits of Tibet,
whose central dwellings are caves. Their ascetic life is severe and
probably comparable to hermitism as it was known in medieval
Europe. It is thought that this Buddhist ideal of sanctity through
the anchorite life spread to Egypt and Syria, and from there to
Europe during the early centuries of Christianity.[49] Hermits and
saints have occasionally been associated with caves in Europe in
the past centuries.

   Like many other cave-hermitages, Einsiedeln has evolved into
a healing shrine, where for many centuries people have come and
found relief from their mental and physical ailments. This is to
say, psychologically, that healing comes from a region outside consciousness, that is, from the unconscious depths. Healing comes
from this unconscious mother, who takes us into her cave so that
new life might be brought forth. The cave represents the darkness and seclusion of the unconscious.[50]

   Movement into the dark regions of the Great Mother and dying for the sake of renewal is beautifully described in Sylvia Perera's

book, *Descent to the Goddess.* Perera describes the Sumerian myth of the descent of Inanna, queen of heaven and earth, into the underworld. During this descent, Inanna must confront the dark goddess, Ereshkigal, who reigns over this region. During her three-day stay, she is killed by Ereshkigal and hung on a peg to rot like a piece of meat. The poem goes on to describe her resurrection and the transformation she experiences through this process. In the end, she is not just the queen of heaven and earth, but one who had descended into the land of the dead and knows its dark mysteries.[51]

From this darkness and seclusion—whether in the caves of the Buddhist anchorites, Inanna in the underworld, or St. Meinrad's hermitage—come the means of psychic-spiritual renewal. At Einsiedeln this process unfolds in context of Christianity, where the risen God-Man, Jesus, enters the cave-tomb as a crucified victim and comes forth as the Risen Savior of Mankind. It is here that mysteries are performed which the mind cannot comprehend, but must simply accept or reject. These are the same mysteries that were celebrated at Eleusis, which took place in a subterranean hall not unlike a cave. The mystery there was also a death-experience from which the community expected its salvation.[52] Whether at Eleusis or at Einsiedeln, the archetypal process of death and rebirth is the same. It is into a cave that each individual must go to find value and meaning to life. Jung comments upon this in his in *Symbols of Transformation:*

> The treasure which the hero fetches from the dark cavern is life: it is himself, new-born from the dark maternal cave of the uncon-scious.[53]

It is beyond argument that the Black Madonna of Einsiedeln has had a tremendous impact on her worshippers, past and present. I have never seen the chapel empty of worshippers on my many trips there. On the walls immediately inside the main entrance (in the direction which the Madonna faces) are a great number of votive offerings in the form of small painted plaques given by people in the past who have felt the impact of the Madonna in their lives. The paintings usually show some crisis, be it sickness or some accident from which they were spared or brought safely through. Off to the sides hang crutches and braces people have left her as thanks after having been cured by her. Like the other black goddesses of Europe, she is associated with healing ability and miracle working. This is usually more common among the black Virgins than among their white counterparts,[54] a fact which accords with the dark, creative and healing forces which lie in the unconscious.

There are many officially recorded reports written in the miracle books of the monastery which testify to miraculous happenings attributed to the Black Madonna.[55] There is little reason to doubt that these miraculous happenings took place. What I am suggesting is that as an archetypal symbol, the Madonna allows for unconscious healing and integration. The power behind an archetype can both destroy and create, enfeeble and restore. The key seems to be in how the archetype, in this case just not the feminine *per se*, but the dark side of the feminine, is able to express itself in the field of everyday reality. The Catholic Church has provided a means of this expression in the person of Mary. In a sense, she is the control valve for a tremendous amount of archetypal power. She is a means through which the archetype of the feminine can find expression at the individual level. When the dark aspect of this archetype is introduced, it too participates in this safety-valve side of Mariology. This is not an impersonal dark feminine force, no matter how it might be defined or expressed. In the case of the Black Madonna, it is a highly cultivated and refined expression of this force that enables her to touch the soul in very personal and meaningful ways, while herself still maintaining a good deal of its impersonal and archetypal nature.

The nature of these miraculous happenings shows that this archetypal force touches in very unexpected ways. The stories might involve, for example, a little boy suddenly talking after having been mute all his life, or a little girl suddenly walking after being crippled for years. There are also reports of people who were giv-en no chance of living but who suddenly recovered their health. The Madonna is held responsible for these sudden changes, for she is the protector of the sick and dying. She is also the guardi-an of the outcast—as evident, for example, in her protection of Jakob Loubi of Baden, who had been imprisoned for slandering the Abbot Gallus of St. Blasien. On the eve of the day he was to be tortured, his chains were suddenly removed. He had a vi-sion of a woman who told him to jump from the window of his cell into a raging river below (a dangerous feat in itself) and make his way for Einsiedeln. The story ends with the charges of slan-der being dropped and Jakob Loubi being exonerated.[56] This is an excellent example in which the collective standard had been challenged by the archetypal force surrounding the Madonna of Einsiedeln. In this story she stands in direct opposition to the senseless suffering of the prisoner, and thus becomes his protectress.

This opposition is readily apparent in other stories, where the sick or suffering are ridiculed for their desire to see the Madonna at Einsiedeln. The implication is that the infirm should rather attempt to find their place in the collective standard. At the same time, when the miraculous takes place, the entire community stands in awe and rejoices. There is an implied passivity here in terms of the collective's recognition and acceptance of the heal-ing power of the Virgin Mother. It literally takes the rejected, infirm and dying to recognize this power and "motherly" intercession into the affairs of a community faced with collective laws and at-titudes. These latter are certainly justifiable in their own right, but not at the expense and suppression of natural healing laws of the unconscious.

What I am suggesting is that the unconscious has its own point of view. What consciousness rejects the unconscious often accepts. In fact, it is often when a person is beaten down, made infirm, imprisoned, or at the point of death, that something new can happen. Though many of the stories are legend, for the most part it seems that they are historically based, though their value lies less in their historicity than in their symbolic spiritual weight. Sickness, imprisonment and impending death are indeed spiritual experiences that grip a person and confront him with the very nature of his destiny. They express themselves in many ways within the psyche, and force individuals to view their lives in ways that are often contradictory to collective standards and viewpoints. As wise as these may be, another wisdom is frequently drawn from such a perspective, transcending the conscious mind and leaving it an astonished witness to events beyond its control and imagination. This is expressed in Christianity in such phrases as "the ways of man not being the ways of God," and "man's justice not being God's justice."

An interesting feature in accounts of miracles is that the Madonna is usually the supplicant's last resort. Conventional remedies are exhausted, hope is given up, and then the suggestion is made to go to "Our Dear Lady of Einsiedeln." This is understandable enough, since we tend to rely on the means at our immediate disposal, *i.e.*, knowledge and insight that has grown with the collective and is, more than likely, valid and time-honored. But when that fails, and everything is stripped away and trivialized, then the unconventional and the unexpected often befalls. This often occurs when every conscious answer and idea is used up; it is then that unconscious forces are given a right to exist. In fact, it is then that the individual often turns to a higher power outside consciousness, whether to a deeper spiritual life or to another individual (or a group). To turn to "Our Dear Lady of Einsiedeln" is a similar idea, turning to the dark healing powers in the maternal unconscious of the psyche.

A final word should be added regarding the festivals and special recognitions around and of the Black Madonna at Einsiedeln. Mention has already been made of the special Pontifical High Mass on the anniversary of St. Meinrad's death, January 21. The two other holidays specific to the Madonna are August 15, the Feast of the Assumption, and September 14, the *Engelweihe* or Feast of the Angelic Dedication of the Lady Chapel. The former is not specific to the Madonna of Einsiedeln, but nevertheless carries a special import, for the simple fact that Einsiedeln is a central European point of pilgrimage. The roots of this festival appear to go back far into pagan history; they recall the great festival of Hecate, the moon goddess of Greece, and of her counterpart, Diana, which in ancient Rome was held annually on August 13. The festival was associated with the harvest, which occurs earlier in the southern countries. The goddesses were asked to spare the crops from storms (which are and were common at that time of the year). During the Feast of the Assumption of Mary, prayers are likewise offered to her to turn aside the storms until the field is ready for harvest.[57] An interesting Syriac text, "The Departure of My Lady Mary from this World," reads:

> And the Apostles also ordered that there should be a commemoration of the Blessed one on the thirteenth of Ab (August), on account of the vines bearing bunches of grapes and on account of the trees bearing fruit, that clouds of hail, bearing stones of wrath, might not come, and the trees be broken, and the fruit, and the vines with their clusters.[58]

This is certainly consistent with the Black Madonna of Einsiedeln and her special concern with the natural order and the vulnerable. As will later be seen, Hecate too had not only a light side but a dark side very much associated with the moon.

The *Engelweihe* of September 14 is peculiar to the Madonna of Einsiedeln. We have already mentioned the background of this festival, which is very important in isolating the Black Madonna as a figure deserving a Chapel all to herself. Thousands of people attend this festival every year, and nearly a million people visit the shrine annually, making it one of the largest pilgrimage centers in Europe. All this emphasizes that the Black Madonna touches a very deep chord in the collective psyche.

It is also interesting to note how the Roman Catholic Church sees her. This is evident in the Indulgences associated with the shrine. The *Engelweihablass*, or Indulgence of Angelic Dedication,

confirmed by Pope Pius VI on May 17, 1793, is granted to all those
who visit the shrine, receive the Sacrament, and pray for the Pope's
intentions. The indulgences one earns at the seven privileged altars of St. Peter's in Rome can be gained by those who visit the
Einsiedeln altars of the Rosary, St. Meinrad, St. Joseph, the Assumption, the Agony in the Garden, St. Benedict and the Patro-
cine altar. This was granted by Pope Leo XIII, September 25, 1889.
The indulgences granted to those who visited the Holy Sepulch-
er in Jerusalem could be gained by all who said the Stations of
the Cross in Einsiedeln. This was granted by Benedict XIV, August 30, 1741. Though there are others, a final interesting one is
that an indulgence of three hundred days is attached to the in-
vocation "Our Lady of Einsiedeln, pray for us," granted by Pope
Pius XI on May 18, 1930." The importance of the Einsiedeln
Madonna is recognized, and testifies to the archetypal power she
embodies.

There is one final special recognition given to the Black Madonna, dating back many centuries, namely the daily singing by the
monks of the *Salve Regina*. This ancient hymn is probably the
most preserved and familiar of the hymns dedicated to the Virgin Mother. Liturgically, it is sung from the end of Pentecost to
the beginning of Advent, the longest season in the Church year.
For this reason alone it would be foremost in the collective consciousness. It truly is a post-resurrectional hymn, bearing both
the agony and pain of human existence, as well as the hope. The
Latin text is presented, along with its translation:

> *Salve, Regina, mater misericordiae; vita, dulcedo et spes nostra, salve.*
> *Ad te clamanus exsules filii Hevae. Ad te suspiramus gementes et flentes*
> *in hac lacrymarum vale. Eia ergo, advocata nostra, illos tuos misericor-*
> *des oculos ad nos converte. Et Jesum, benedictum fructum vintris bui*
> *nobis post hoc exsilium ostende. O Clemens, O Pia, O Dulcis Virgo*
> *Maria.*
>
> *Hail, Holy Queen,* mother of mercy, our life, our sweetness and
> our hope. To thee do we cry, poor banished children of Eve. To
> thee do we send up our sighs, mourning and weeping in this val-

ley of tears. Turn then, our advocate, your eyes of mercy toward
us. And after this, our exile, show unto us the blessed fruit of
thy womb, Jesus. O Clement, O Loving, O Sweet Virgin Mary.

Detail is not necessary at this point, except to suggest that such
a hymn captures the human situation for countless people. The
subtle twist here is that she not only touches those in the valley
of tears, she *is* the valley of tears. She is life with all of its entan-
glements. Without this entanglement life would have no drama—if
indeed we would even be able to speak of it, it would be one-
dimensional and sterile. Such a recognition leads an individual
more fully into the compensatory darkness of the feminine in an
age that is too often prone to devalue the human predicament
and to sentimentalize to an extent that nearly borders on the mor-
bid. This hymn is an appeal for life's energy to move on within
the valley of tears in such a way that meaning and value can be
given to the senseless sufferings of mankind. It is not, nor should
it be, an appeal for release.

Chapter Three—Notes

[1]A. Schmid, *Corolla Heremitana: Neue Beiträge zur Kunst und Geschichte Einsiedelns und der Innerschweiz* (Festgabe für L. Berchler), 1964, p. 134

[2]From the *Rollwagenbüchlein* by Jörg Wickram from Kolmar in Elsass, the town clerk who recorded it in 1555. To this day it is the only report concerning the origins of the Madonna at Einsiedeln (my translation from the original)

[3]Erich Neumann, *The Great Mother*, p. 310

[4]*Ibid.*, p. 320

[5]*Ibid.*

[6]C.G. Jung, *Aion* (*CW* IX, ii), Chapter 5

[7]C.G. Jung, *CW* XIV, p. 18

[8]Neumann, p. 30

[9]*Wallfahrtsgeschichte*, p. 35

[10]One of the monks I spoke with said that there was no meaning to it, which partially suggests the insignificance placed on it.

[11]Leviticus 8: 23-24; Exodus 29:20

[12]C.G. Jung, *CW* V, p. 123

[13]*Ibid.*, p. 124

[14]*Man, Myth and Magic*, Vol. V, p. 2120

[15]*Ibid.*, Vol. III, p. 966

[16]C.G. Jung, *CW* V, p. 124

[17]*Ibid.*, p. 352

[18]*Man, Myth and Magic*, Vol. VII, p. 2985

[19]*Tannhäuser im Venusberg*, p. 147

[20]*Ibid.*, p. 54. My translation.

[21]C.G. Jung, *CW* V, p. 412

[22]A *Dictionary of Symbols*, p. 136

[23]For a thorough treatment of this myth, see A.N. Ammann's *Tannhäuser im Venusberg*

[24]C.G. Jung, CW XIV, p. 356

[25]C.G. Jung, CW XIII, p. 269

[26]C.G. Jung, CW XIV, p. 511

[27]C.G. Jung, CW IX, i, p. 314

[28]C.G. Jung, CW XIV, pp. 27-28

[29]Ibid, p. 28. Jung is citing the "Consilium coniugli" from the alchemical text *Ars chemica*

[30]*Ibid.*, p. 29

[31]*Ibid.*

[32]C.G. Jung, CW XI, p. 249

[33]Andrea Dykes, *Medusa's Influence Today* (unpub. diss.), p. 143

[34]*Encyclopedia of Religion and Ethics*, p. 536

[35]A *Dictionary of Symbols*, p. 135

[36]*Man, Myth and Magic*, Vol. III, p. 1237

[37]*Encyclopedia of Religion and Ethics*, p. 536

[38]C.G. Jung, CW XIV, p. 513

[39]Dykes, p. 107

[40]Four is a numerical symbol of wholeness; sixteen (four times four) would thus represent a refined and very differentiated expression of this wholeness

[41]Neumann, p. 184

[42]*Ibid.*

[43]*Ibid.*

[44]For a very good analogy between the solar cycle and human life, see Jung's *Symbols of Transformation* (CW V), pp. 355-357

[45]Neumann, p. 174

[46]C.G. Jung, *CW* V, p. 338

[47]C.G. Jung, *CW* IX, i, p. 135

[48]*Ibid.*

[49]*Encyclopedia of Religion and Ethics*, p. 267

[50]C.G. Jung, *CW* XII, p. 153

[51]See Sylvia Perera, *Descent to the Goddess*

[52]Neumann, p. 318

[53]C.G. Jung, *CW* V, p. 374

[54]Esther Harding, *Woman's Mysteries*, p. 109

[55]*Madonna im Finstern Wald*, Part III, pp. 58-102

[56]*Ibid.*, pp. 59-63

[57]Harding, p. 112

[58]*Ibid.*

[59]*Our Lady of Hermits*, pp. 36-3

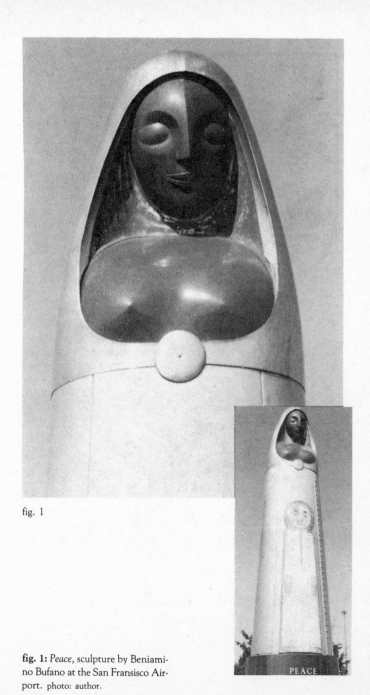

fig. 1

fig. 1: *Peace*, sculpture by Beniamino Bufano at the San Fransisco Airport. photo: author.

fig. 2

fig. 2: The Einsiedeln Coat of
Arms: Two Ravens. fig. 3: Twelfth
Century miniature. Cod. 111 of
Einsiedeln Library. photo: P. Damian
Rutishauser.

fig. 3

fig. 4

fig. 4: The Black Madonna of Einsiedeln. photo: P. Damian Rutishauser. **fig. 5:** The Black Madonna of Einsiedeln and the casket containing the skull of St. Meinrad. photo: Kartenverlag J. Eberle. **fig. 6:** The Black Madonna of Einsiedeln showing the leaved sceptor. photo: Kartenverlag J. Eberle.

fig. 5

fig. 7

fig. 7: The Black Madonna of Einsiedeln detail showing clouds and lightning. **fig. 8:** Chapel of the Black Madonna. photo: Kartenverlag J. Eberle.

fig. 8

fig. 9

fig. 9: Kali, from Heinrich Zimmer's *Myths and Symbols in Indian Art and Civilization.* **fig. 10:** Kali standing on Shiva/Shava, from Heinrich Zimmer's *Myths and Symbols in Indian Art and Civilization.*

fig. 10

fig. 11: Artemis the "Many Breasted," from *Ancient Pagan and Modern Christian Symbolism* by Thomas Inman, 1876.

fig. 12: *The Immaculate Conception of 1749,* by D. Pozzi, outside the cathedral at Einsiedeln. photo: author.

fig. 13: *Black Madonna Beneath the Streets of Chicago*

fig. 14: Black mother,
fig. 15: Two big black hands

fig. 15

fig. 14

4

OTHER GODDESSES OF DARKNESS

The Black Madonna of Einsiedeln is not an isolated entity. Though she is certainly unique in her own way, she is not unrelated to the world of mythology and comparative religion. This is essentially so because of her archetypal nature, which necessitates her "belonging" to the thousands of expressions of the feminine archetype throughout the world, though more specifically to the dark side of that archetype. Such belonging must not be understood as mitigating the psychic-spiritual power specific to the Black Madonna of Einsiedeln, but rather the reverse. It is a broadening of her psychic-spiritual base to relate her to the universal laws which govern the human psyche and aptly express themselves in mythologies and religions throughout the world. Such a belonging then becomes her enrichment. It is the intent of this chapter, then, to lift the dark virgin from her specific context at Einsiedeln and place her in relationship to other goddesses throughout the world who are associated with darkness.

Kali

Perhaps the most dramatic, striking and dark of these goddesses is Kali of India. If the Madonna of Einsiedeln can be said to be touched with a sense of charm and grace, then Kali would be her exact counterpart (see figure nine). Beyond this first impression, however, the two goddesses do have some elements in common.

The name Kali means "black." In Vedic days this name was associated with the god Agni (fire), who had seven flickering tongues of flame for devouring oblations of butter. Of these seven, Kali was the "black" or "terrible" tongue. This association is essentially lost, but it developed into the goddess Kali, who is considered to be the fierce and bloody consort of Shiva.[1] Shiva and Shakti represent the opposites of masculine and feminine energies, which together are manifestations of the neuter Brahman in Hindu mythology; Kali is the fierce, dark dimension of the Shakti feminine energy.

The Absolute expresses itself in these two figures, and life is seen as an interplay between them. Shakti, the female side of the Absolute, is both creative and destructive, though it is because of her fiercer side that she is especially worshipped in India.[2] As mother, she is both life-nourishing and ever-destructive. This latter side of Shakti is known as Kali; she is the terrifying side of the Shakti principle and gives not only shape and reality to life, but also its vital energy.[3]

Kali is often portrayed with very ugly features, bloodshot eyes, matted hair and black skin. She wears a necklace of human skulls and a belt of human teeth. She has long fangs and a protruding tongue. Sometimes she holds a rope to strangle her victims. Her other two hands are often raised in a gesture of encouragement or blessing, thus suggesting her paradoxical nature. She is held responsible for smallpox, plague, cholera and the high fevers before death. Blood sacrifices to her were common in the past and are still an essential part of her worship today. She is known as *Nitya-Kali* (The Everlasting Black One), *Smasana-Kali* (Kali of the Cremation Ground), *Raksa-Kali* (Goblin Kali), and *Syama-Kali* (Dark Kali).[4] Her name is also reflected in the Hindu concept of the world cycles. Each world cycle is subdivided into four *yu-gas* or world stages. The last of these is the Kali Yuga, the Dark Age, in which *Dharma,* or the power and essentiality of right-eousness, is only one quarter as strong as it had been in the earli-est, most righteous, and most lengthy of the four ages, the Krita Yuga. The Kali Yuga, the shortest and most decadent of the *yu-gas,* lasts only 432,000 years.

A most dramatic representation of the nature of Kali is seen in figure nine. Here, the paradoxical nature mentioned above is obvious. In one hand she holds the severed head of a victim, and a sword in the other—presumably the instrument of killing. Her two other hands represent bounty, one holding a bowl of food, the other simply extended in a gesture of offering. She is dancing on her consort Shiva. Though there is certainly a note of terror and horror in this picture, there are still points of similarity be-tween her and the Black Madonna of Einsiedeln.

In addition to their similarity of color, both figures are associated with the human head. What the Madonna suggests implicitly, Kali emphasizes explicitly. She wants heads, that is, sacrifices. She craves blood offerings. Indeed, before her, the seat of judgment, the head, is cut off and proven impotent. What she offers is be-yond the human intellect. As already suggested, the Madonna expresses this same theme. The head of St. Meinrad is held in high reverence, not just as a sign of martyrdom but as a symbol of the direction psychic transformation must take. The head must be sacrificed, that is, the intellect must be cut off. Whether one stands before Kali or the Madonna of Einsiedeln, the effect is the same, namely that the rational mind loses its ability to explain the dark uncanny forces of life as they are experienced within and without the psyche. These are, practically speaking, those unexplainable "black" experiences of life which most individuals would just as well do without and in which there seems to be little or no value. The Madonna of Einsiedeln holds the scepter which simply shows how those dark forces that can determine a person's destiny have their own irrational power. Yet Kali has a scepter of her own—a sword. She is much more direct and crude; with her, nothing is hidden. She is very clear about her victim; it is the head she holds in her left hand. The Madonna, too, holds a victim of sorts in her left arm—the infant Jesus. The parallel is subtle but no less real. There is a dual aspect to both Kali and the Madonna. Kali is certainly the terrible destroying mother first and foremost, while the Madonna is primarily the loving, caring and gentle mother. Yet Kali, too, can be a loving mother. Sri Ramakrishna, a nineteenth-century Tantric philosopher, expresses the paradox:

> To my Divine Mother I prayed only for pure love, I offered flowers at Her Lotus feet and prayed to Her: "Mother, here is Thy virtue, here is Thy vice. Take them both and grant me only pure love for Thee. Here is Thy knowledge, here is Thy ignorance. Take them both and grant me only pure love for Thee. Here is Thy purity, here is Thy impurity. Take them both, Mother, and grant me only pure love for Thee. Here is Thy dharma, here is Thy adharma. Take them both, Mother, and grant me only pure love for Thee."[5]

For her part, Mary has been largely deprived of the dark destroying side of the feminine. Yet the dual nature of the Virgin Mary is reflected in depictions of her not only as the Lord's mother but, according to some medieval allegories, as his cross.[6] In our own time, this dark side is more clearly and graphically apparent in those rare instances where a black Virgin Mary has arisen. In such places, the community around her is often made up of people who have a vital relationship to the earth and are touched by the blood and guts of a history—now a living mythology sustaining their very being. One notable example is Our Lady of Czestochowa in Poland: Lech Walesa has stated that she is the power behind him and Solidarity; armbands with her picture on them have been worn by participants in the movement. Whenever the dark side of one of these figures has been developed, however, the effect is nowhere near that of Kali. Yet at the same time, this side of life is then given at least a measure of expression to

compensate for the too one-sided "white" and pure aspect of the
Virgin Mother, and for those cultural attitudes that need to keep
her that way.

The duality of the maternal archetype is expressed in its loving
and terrible aspects. The negative side of this archetype is defined
by Jung as

> . . . anything secret, hidden, dark; the abyss, the world of the dead,
> anything that devours, seduces, that poisons, that is terrifying and
> inescapable like fate.[7]

In this light it could be suggested that perhaps the East, notably
India, has a better grasp of this side of life and thus dares to have
a relationship with it, to the point of "loving" it. Such a view is
in general beyond the imagination of the West. On this point Jung
says that:

> It seems as if the development of the feeling function in Western
> man forced a choice on him which led to the moral splitting of
> the divinity into two halves. In the East the predominantly intui-
> tive intellectual attitude left no room for feeling values, and the
> gods—Kali is a case in point—could retain their original paradox-
> ical morality undisturbed. Thus Kali is representative of the East
> and the Madonna of the West. The latter has entirely lost the
> shadow that still distantly followed her in the allegories of the
> Middle Ages. It was relegated to the hell of popular imagination,
> where it now leads an insignificant existence as the devil's grand-
> mother.[8]

The paradoxical nature of Kali is graphically expressed in figure
ten, a Tantric representation of her standing on Shiva-Shava. All
around are bones and skulls. Animals are feasting on the remains.
Some divinities from the Hindu pantheon are looking on in terror from the background. Kali is typically black. She wears her
usual wreath of severed heads. One right hand holds a sword and
the other right hand a pair of scissors to cut the thread of life.
But in her left hands she holds a bowl and the lotus symbol of
eternal generations. She stands on two Shiva figures, one on top

of the other. The lower one is a bearded naked ascetic who lies as if dead, because he does not touch the feet of the goddess.[9] On top of him is a counterpart who is stirring slightly and seemingly coming to life. This is so because he is in full contact with Shakti in the form of Kali. Shakti is thus both the life-giving and life-taking energy. She is the embodiment of its very essence.[10]

It was believed that one could not be a successful Tantric until one deeply understood the meaning behind Kali. Rituals in her honor were often performed in cemeteries and among corpses. Such rituals were intended to help a person integrate the horrible aspects of life—all considered essential to a deeper understanding of the processes of life, a practically insuperable difficulty for the Western mind. Yet this may be the growing edge for those of us of the West—to understand consciously the shadow sides of life, which in turn would give dimension and depth to what would otherwise be a one-sided, unblemished and moralistic perspective.

Perhaps part of our predicament in the West, collectively and individually, is that most of us do not participate in the shadow side of life and thus fall victim to it unconsciously in such a way that the most incredible kinds of atrocities are committed. By refusing to accept inherent evil in ourselves, we commit it and project it. Unconsciousness of our shadow can indeed be a destructive matter. Kali may be only a stone's throw, issue-wise, from our present Western situation, but she does suggest that the dark, seemingly destroying side of life exists and accordingly must find a place in our attitudes and existential outlook. What she embodies must be more consciously integrated into the Western psyche.

Like so many ruling earth-goddesses, Kali reflects the order of life. Here, according to Erich Neumann, "cruelty, death, and caprice stand side by side with supreme planning, perfect purposiveness, and immortal life."[11] Blackness can then reflect a psychological attitude well grounded in human experience; but then it also becomes relative. Sri Ramakrishna, in reply to a question regarding the blackness of Kali, said:

> Is Kali, my Divine Mother, of a black complexion? She appears black because She is viewed from a distance, but when intimately known She is no longer so. The sky appears blue at a distance; but when you go near and take it in your hand, you find that it is colorless.[12]

Heinrich Zimmer gives an interesting background of the dynamics of Kali's personality. The energy of life is both destructive and creative and, in fact, are one and the same process:

> Life feeds on life. In the end, every creature becomes food for another. The aging and dying generation is to be replaced by the younger. She gives to one and takes from another.[13]

The name Kali means not only "black"; it is also the feminine form of the word *Kala*, meaning "time." Time brings in and ushers out. Kali, like life, hungers for life. None truly escape her. She appears in the psyche as the unpredictable shadowy feminine side of the unconscious, the "terror that underlies every activity."[14] She is the dread side of life in whatever manner it can menace us. In the end, however, such sides of life make a justifiable claim on our psyche. In Heinrich Zimmer's words,

> To us of the West, brought up under the shadow of the Gothic Cathedral, where the benign figure of the Blessed Mother, immaculate, is uncontaminated by the darker principle...—India's Mother, eternal India's horrific-beautiful, caressing-murdering symbolization of the totality of the world creating-destroying eating-eaten one, seems more than difficult to love. Yet, we can discover if we will pause—something that will speak to us of a wonder beyond beauty and ugliness, a peace balancing the terms of birth and death.[15]

Without Kali, and the same principle is reflected in the Black Madonna, the psyche would not be stirred to its deepest levels. In one respect, she inhibits consciousness by threatening and destroying what can be called ego consciousness. Yet without her there would be no motivation and challenge to a higher consciousness. Without her there are no heroes. Life would come to a standstill.

Isis

Kali is blackness magnified to its crudest degree, and as such personifies those terrible stirrings and forces in the psyche that seem like death to an individual, but which in the end turn out to be part of the vital process needed to transform life into something of greater value and meaning. Yet to the average Westerner, Kali is too distant and unapproachable. Grace and charm are not her strengths. Much more accessible and nearer to conscious acceptance is a goddess such as Isis of Egypt. She too, like Kali, is not only the creator mother and nurse of all, but also the destroyer. She is often depicted as a black woman holding her infant son, Horus, in her arms.[16] A very good description of her can be found in the dream of Lucius in Apuleius' *Golden Ass.*

> First, she had a great abundance of haire, dispersed and scattered about her neck, on the crown of her head she bare many garlands and interlaced with flowers, in the middle of her forehead was a compass in fashion of a glasse, or resembling the light of the Moone, in one of her hands she bare serpents, in the other, blades of corne, her vestiment was of fine silke yielding divers colors, sometime yellow, sometime rosie, sometime flamy, and sometime (which troubled my spirit sore) darke and obscure, covered with blacke robe in manner of a shield, and pleated in most subtill fashion at the skirts of her garments, the welts appeared comely, whereas here and there the stars glimpsed, and in the middle of them was placed the Moon, which shone like a flame of fire, round about the robe was a coronet or garland made with flowers and fruit.[17]

Such a description aptly presents Isis as the Mother who embodies all aspects within herself. Beneath her exterior black robe she is multicolored. She wears a garland of flowers on her head, as well as an image of the moon. She is thus related to life and love and the dim light of the night. The stars cover her black robe. She is very much like the Queen of the Night in Mozart's *The Magic Flute*; Mozart was very much interested in the story behind this opera which, in many ways, plays on the theme of

Isis as Queen of the Night (a figure of concern in Freemasonry).

Isis is a lady of the underworld, which is not unlike the deep recesses of the unconscious psyche. Dr. Marie-Louise von Franz has given us a very good description of the mythological function of Isis.[18] Within the world-structure of ancient Egyptian religious tradition, there is both a Sun principle and an Isis feminine principle. The former is a trinity consisting of the sun god, Ra, or his earthy representative the Pharaoh; a generating principle known as *Ka-mutef*, which means "the bull of his mother," by which the king is able to generate his son and successor; and the Prince, the third member of the trinity. The fourth is missing, yet is expressed in the Isis feminine principle. She is excluded from the light, sun principle of life.

The Isis feminine principle is also a trinity, consisting first of Osiris, who is not only the husband of Isis, but also the secret ruler of the underworld.[19] He is comparable to the Self or center of the psyche which stands behind the Isis principle. He, in von Franz's definition, is the "personification of the collective unconscious, all that existed in the collective unconscious psyche, but which was not included in the conscious religious forms of that time."[20] The second member is Seth, brother of Isis and murderer of Osiris. He is evil, the murdering destroying side of the Isis principle. As such, he also stands against the sun god, Ra. The third member is Thot, a baboon god who is a counterpart to *Ka-mutef* and embodies a spirit of wisdom peculiar to this trinity. He is the wisdom of the unconscious.

The bridge between these two principles is Horus, the son of Osiris. After Seth killed Osiris, he cut his body up and threw it in the Nile. Isis recovered all of the parts except his phallus. In grief, she fashioned one out of wood and impregnated herself. From this she gave birth to Horus, thus giving rebirth to Osiris. With her love she brought forth again the potency of her dead husband. Osiris is the new sun god or a renewed sun-principle, and the means by which life is renewed on earth.

The Egyptian trinitarian concept is important and interesting in two respects. First, it gives a good conceptual picture of the very same phenomenon in Christianity, where a trinitarian masculine godhead has in effect excluded the feminine principle.[21] The matter of the missing fourth applies as much to Egyptian mythology as it does to Christianity. Though this is also reflected in the Madonna of Einsiedeln, it does not reflect an issue peculiar to her, even though she graphically emphasizes it. This is seen by her location in the western end of the Church, her femininity, her blackness, and her unpredictable character.

More related to the issue at hand, however, is the other aspect of the trinitarian concept, namely, what it reveals about the Isis feminine principle *per se*. The trinity is made up of Osiris, Seth, and Thot. This is to say that the feminine principle contains the Self; behind her lies the center of the personality, ". . .that aspect of the unconscious which reveals itself as the nucleus of the total personality. . ."[22] This is both within and behind her. She also contains Seth, a murdering, destructive side that is completely opposed to consciousness (Ra). Consciousness experiences any loss on its part as death. We have already mentioned that the Black Madonna is associated with death through her westerly direction and her relation to the skull. She is the extinguisher of consciousness, or of collective conscious norms and attitudes. She shares the less subtle nature of Kali and the more approachable form of Isis. Seth is a side of Isis that, if left to its own devices, would even destroy the symbol of the Self, Osiris. But neither Isis nor the unconscious can tolerate this, since the unconscious wishes to relate to outer reality. It wishes to give birth, to generate and come alive in the world of mankind. The unconscious has not only a blood tie to the destroying aspect of life, but is also a mother who gives birth and nourishes into a higher consciousness.

The other aspect of Isis, Thot, clearly emphasizes her uncanny nature. Thot is baboon-like, that is, full of unexpected tricks. At the same time, the baboon represents a more critical mind in the world of animals.[23] Thot represents a nature-wisdom that often counterposes collective insights. All three, Osiris, Seth, and Thot, are aspects of Isis—and like the unconscious, hold the secret of the Self, are often experienced as terribly dark and frightening, and have a truly uncanny and unpredictable nature.

From such an underworld trinity, however, a child is born—Horus, a new consciousness born from death. This theme has already been mentioned in connection with Kali and the Black Madonna, who holds the Child in her arms. Consciousness is in the arms of the unconscious, which both gives it life and destroys it. The Pharaoh at death is no longer Horus, but Osiris, only to have the process repeated again and again. Consciousness is continually renewed through the process of death and rebirth. The wisdom of Isis is not that of the sun principle or of Logos, but rather a wisdom of things as they are. Her name means "ancient," and as *Maat*, she is "Knowledge" or "Wisdom"—thus she is "ancient wisdom."[24] To Plutarch, Isis was both wise and philosophic. According to R.E. Witt,

> A very important bridge between paganism and Christianity was the speculative system of the Hellenizing Jew Philo of Alexandria and in it the cornerstone was "Holy Wisdom" (*Hagia Sophia*), Mother of the divine Logos, rightly identified with Isis; Isis-Sophia could be thought to produce Harpocrates as the Logos.[25]

Harpocrates is the Greek name for Horus the Child. This is just another way of saying that all consciousness comes from the unconscious side of the psyche, which operates from a perspective of wisdom peculiar to itself alone.

The wisdom of Isis is of another order than that of Logos. As a result, Isis embodies a generative power that is able to reincarnate Osiris in the form of Horus. Through her love she gives him back his life;[26] in the mysteries of Isis, the initiate sought to become Osiris and thus be raised from the dead.[27] With such power, Isis is associated with healing, much as is the Black Madonna. Isis is interested in healing the body. To all who need her help, she appears in dreams. She also brewed a medicine called *moly*, which is not unlike the *soma* or *hoama* drink in Persian and Hindu sources. This drink is able to revive the dead and even, in the case of Horus, grant immortality.[28] Isis was considered the "wonder worker with the gift of healing the sick."[29] The process of healing often involved incantations and spells against the disease. The spellbinder would take a piece of pitch and make a sacrifice facing the moon. Words were then spoken to Isis: "Thy kingdom resides in that which is utterly black."[30] Like the Madonna of Einsiedeln, Isis too is considered a virgin, the Mother of God, and as we have now seen, the "black" healer.

But why black? The answer is commonly given in associating this with the dark, earthy, healing side of the unconscious. A finer distinction here, however, lies in the consideration that Isis was black during the period of her mourning. She became black-robed and herself black complexioned. This mourning is significant in relationship to her healing side. The myth says that she mourns for Osiris, who has been killed and dismembered. Plutarch says that

> The horned ones of her [Isis] statues are representations of her crescent, while by the blackrobed ones are signified the occultations and overshadowings in which she follows the Sun [Osiris], looking after him.[31]

This seems to correspond to the winter solstice, when the sun (Osiris) is farthest away. Isis, the embodiment of life itself, goes in search of her husband; she is the golden cow covered with black.[32] One of her priestly groups known as the "Wearers of Black" specialized in the mourning side of Isis,[33] especially that which mourns after the Sun (Osiris) principle. With the resurrection of Osiris through Horus, life could go on, but mourning was recognized as an essential part of the worship of Isis.

This mourning is important psychologically, for it intimates that the black unconscious side of the soul is not static. It mourns after consciousness and is not content until it finds it. When it does find the pieces of consciousness, it too, like Isis, gives it back its life, nourishes it and helps to bring it to a fullness of its own. Consciousness may indeed become dismembered, or, one could say, dissociated. It can break into a thousand pieces, leaving a person with a sense of emptiness and despair—a true black night of the soul. But the black night is not meant to be continual, though this certainly can happen. Isis does not wish to be black permanently, for she also wears under her outer black garment a coat of many colors. It seems that the unconscious seeks healing, restoration, a new life. This mourning is a critical psychological point; it implies striving after and searching for a new life. Unconsciousness seeks a reconciliation with, or perhaps more correctly, rebirth into consciousness. Such a birth is indeed essentially related to any basic notion one might have of healing. The Black Madonna of Einsiedeln in all her blackness and queenliness carries this very same theme, though the mourning aspect is far less overt and is only occasionally hinted at, as in the *Salve Regina:* "mourning and weeping in this valley of tears."

The Moon

Of all the natural phenomena, none seems to capture the twofold mystery of maleness and femaleness as well as the relationship of sun and moon. The sun stands with all of its bright consistency as that aggressive force which pushes its way through the heavens, rising and dying with the coming and passing of each day. It exposes all in its light, fertilizes the earth with its energy, discriminates by making visible, and, following the true masculine Logos principle, touches the world not only with its revelations, but often with its non-subtle, overly harsh penetrating light.

The moon, on the other hand, is a very appropriate symbol for the feminine world.[34] It is the Lesser Light which rules the night with its shadowy reflections and subtle blendings. As the sun rules the light of consciousness, the moon rules the night of unconsciousness, of instincts and of the inner intuitive world.[35] The moon has long been considered a beneficient feminine deity throughout the world. The ancients believed the moon was the gathering place of the dead, the storehouse of the seed of life and, accordingly, a feminine being.[36] It was, and is, considered indispensable to life and growth. To worship the moon was to pay homage to the creative and fertilizing powers of nature; the moon was considered the repository of a special wisdom of the natural order, of instincts, and of the full processes of life and death. This is especially emphasized because the moon waxes and wanes. Though the sun rises and falls, the moon changes more gradually and subtly, and thus is more consistent with those deeper mysterious forces of life. To worship the sun, on the other hand, is to worship "that which overcomes nature, which orders her chaotic fullness and harnesses her powers to the fulfilling of man's ends."[37]

The moon, in its transformations and flux, reflects in a most dramatic way the same fluctuations within the psyche. The moon increases and decreases, and so too the inner world peculiar to us all. There is both the light waxing side of the psyche and a dark waning side. Both are necessary for that mysterious balance without which there is no human drama, growth, dimension or imagination.

The moon is often symbolized by a crescent, which can be either on the increase or decrease, though usually the former. Both the waxing and waning crescents are potent and related to growth and change. The waxing moon was especially related to growth and, indeed, was even considered responsible for it[38]; the word *crescent*, in fact, comes from the Latin word *crescere*, which means "to grow."[39] And yet the waning moon is also a crescent, and is thus an agent of growth, though growth in its dark aspect, which is usually unrecognized until much later.

The power of the declining moon resounds strikingly in Greek mythology. In the earliest days, the moon was simply known as Selene. With time she split into Aphrodite, the bright moon, and Hecate, the dark. Still later, the moon was simply called "Hecate-the-Three-Headed," which referred to its three phases—Artemis the crescent or waxing moon, Selene the full moon, and Hecate the waning or dark moon. The interesting feature here is that all three phases can be represented by Hecate the dark moon[40]; for the Greeks, the power of life lay in the darkness of the moon. It is said that Aphrodite, the bright Moon, taught her son Jason how to "draw down the dark moon" when he needed the help of magic powers.[41] Though she did not have this magic, she knew that Hecate did. Hecate had at her disposal potent healing and destructive substances.[42] Thus the dark side of the moon represents not only the destructive sides of life, but also those necessary forces that make creativity, growth, and healing possible. The moon is the goddess of storms and fertility, both without and within the psyche. According to Esther Harding, "Magic, inspiration, and understanding are her gifts."[43] Further,

> Their [the ancients] supreme deity was like the moon, not like the sun. She was dual in her very nature. She lived her life in phases, manifesting the qualities of each phase in turn. In the upperworld phase, corresponding to the bright moon, she is good, kind, and beneficent. In the other phase, corresponding to the time when the moon is dark, she is cruel, destructive, and evil. It is not that these goddesses are undifferentiated or unreliable. For as, from the first day when the slender crescent appears in the sky, it can be relied on to increase in size and brightness, night by night, till the full moon, and there-after to decrease, until the brightness of the moon "has been eaten up" by the dark moon, so the goddess turns first her beneficent face and then her angry aspect towards men.[44]

This is a beautiful recognition of the two forces always operating in life, a dynamic which the moon graphically portrays.

It is more difficult for us to accept this contradictory nature than it was for primitive peoples; our more rational mind cannot easily tolerate such a flux. Yet both the light and dark poles are always present, no matter how neatly one or the other may be covered. Both are always at work and indispensable to the mysterious round of life and death, growth and decay. Both represent a counterbalance in life, as the moon goddess Diana, or Artemis the "Many Breasted," displays in figure eleven. Both the light and dark sides—that is, the waxing and waning sides of the moon—offer nourishment. There are countless moon goddesses throughout the world who express, in one way or another, this same theme.

Close to the Western ethos is Mary herself. Of her many titles in the Litany to Mary, one is "Moon." Mary is the Moon of the Church, while Christ is the Sun. Innocent III (Pope from 1198-1216) said of Mary:

> Towards the Moon it is he should look, who is buried in the shadow of sin and iniquity. Having lost divine grace, the day disappears, there is no more sun for him; but the Moon is still in the horizon. Let him address himself to Mary; under her influence thousands every day find their way to God.⁴⁵

In other words, the feminine principle is to be sought out even over against the masculine-sun-conscious principle.

Though Mary is not consciously understood to be a moon goddess, she nevertheless bears the same archetypal significance as her predecessors. If this were not so, one would wonder why she is even called the "Moon" at all, though in most cases the light and dark sides of the moon are not clearly associated with her. The Black Madonna of Einsiedeln and others like her throughout Europe are distinct exceptions: here the dark side comes through and with the same meaning as Hecate-the-Three-Headed. The Madonna of Einsiedeln is a healing goddess simply because she is black. She is associated with the moon, as was seen earlier in the consecration of the original Holy Chapel. The early woodcuts did not fail to show an open window with the stars and the moon (a crescent) shining through. In addition, the statue of the Immaculate Conception of 1749 by D. Pozzi outside the Cathedral at Einsiedeln and standing inside the Lady Fountain shows Mary standing on the crescent moon, crushing a serpent at the same time (figure twelve). In effect, Mary is both the crescent and the dragon. On her face is a look of anguish, for as the title of the statue implies, she has been impregnated—she is to be the bearer of the seed of new spiritual truth and power. For this, she must suppress or, in fact, transform her dragon side. She is now not the destroyer but the bearer and nourisher of life. What must not be forgotten, however, is that her dragon-destroying side is not dead, and will emerge at some future point if not consciously integrated soon.

Mary as the moon is little different than the association of Isis with the moon as described by Apuleius (see above, p.80). Both figures are strikingly similar to the description given in the twelfth chapter of the book of Revelation to John:

> And a great portent appeared in heaven, a woman clothed with the sun, with the moon under her feet, and on her head a crown of twelve stars; she was with child and she cried out in her pangs of birth, in anguish for delivery. And another portent appeared in heaven; behold, a great red dragon, with seven heads and ten horns, and seven diadems upon his heads. His tail swept down a third of the stars of heaven, and cast them to the earth. And the dragon stood before the woman who was about to bear a child, that he might devour her child when she brought it forth; she brought forth a male child, one who is to rule all the nations with a rod of iron, but her child was caught up to God and to his throne, and the woman fled into the wilderness, where she has a place prepared by God, in which to be nourished for one thousand two hundred and sixty days.[46]

It is also acknowledged that God has prepared a place for this Queen of the Night; in other words, she is a part of the total plan for life. Though banished, the feminine archetype is very much alive. She is pregnant with life and meaning, just as the unconscious is often pregnant with lifesaving contents. Such a reading also psychologically predicts the return of the feminine principle from the unconscious through the nourishing wilderness of the soul for men and women alike.[47]

Psychological insight into the nature of the moon is important for a more thorough understanding of the Black Madonna of Einsiedeln. The cool soft light of the moon compensates the bright light of the sun. In a time when the mind has claimed ascendancy in nearly every area of life, it becomes necessary to be reminded that the soul is not a mere container that can be emptied and analyzed according to our own perspectives and prejudices. The sun of consciousness must give way to the moon of unconsciousness.

The Madonna of Einsiedeln and others like her reflect this vital need. It is not enough just to say that we need a renewed relationship to the feminine in our times. What is needed is a relationship to the *dark* side of the feminine. On one hand, the Moon is the Queen of the Night and represents that which is cold, dark, and moist. It hides from the light of day, from man's enlightened thinking, and, accordingly, holds the secret of life.[48] On the other hand, the secret of life lies not just in the ascendant moon but also in the descendent phase. Indeed, it could be conjectured that for our times especially, when so much emphasis is placed on the good, sweet, beautiful, perfect and sentimental, secrets of life may just well lie on the descendent side. The dark moon leads to the underworld but, accordingly, makes transformation possible.[49] Like Inanna in the Sumerian myth, descent to and death in the underworld ultimately leads us to transformation and renewal. Inanna was forced to confront the dark goddess, Ereshkigal, who like the dark moon holds the power to "destroy or create and heal—depending on what attitude we take" towards this dark side of the feminine.[50] And, in the words of Esther Harding,

> . . .we must recognize that, although the road of the crescent leads downward, yet it also may lead to transformation of the personality, to a real rebirth of the individual.[51]

The dark moon side of our psyches becomes today the region of individual salvation. The unconscious holds the secrets of renewal—secrets which are often diametrically opposed to conscious viewpoints.

Consciousness need not be a victim but rather a listener. To follow conscious logic through to its own end leads to nonsense—

there can be no such thing as an unending day, since night must come. There can be no such thing as total revelation in consciousness, for the secrets of life can never nor ought ever be *all* revealed; wholeness is impossible without the recognition of shadow and free will. The night exists; shadow exists; unconsciousness exists. Resolution lies in seeing that the moon side of our psyche, that is, the unconscious, offers a special kind of value for us all—again, in Harding's words: ". . . an ever-renewed life like the moon's own, in which diminishing and dying are as essential as becoming."[52] Creation and destruction, birth and death, growth and decay, conscious and unconscious, are vital aspects of one total process within and without the psyche. The Black Madonna of Einsiedeln beckons one to such an unorthodox understanding. That such a need is so greatly felt, if only unconsciously, is one reason it seems that so many pilgrimages are made to her every year. Though she does not intend to fight the wisdom of the Father, she certainly offers a special wisdom of her own, which itself can be experienced in the depths of the psyche.

Demeter and Kore

The transformative properties of the moon have a more specific parallel with the mysteries associated with the Greek myth of Demeter and her daughter Kore (maiden), better known as Persephone, the maiden of the spring. One day when she was out in a field, she was carried away by the Lord of the Underworld, Hades, who took her down into his kingdom below the earth. Demeter, finding no trace of her, roamed the earth for nine days until she came to the Sun, who told her of her daughter's fate. Demeter mourned and nothing grew. In the end, Zeus intervened and made an agreement that Persephone would spend a portion of her time on earth and another portion in the underworld. These periods of time correspond to the blossoming forth of nature (Persephone's return) and its eventual death (her death). Though the story can be told with much more complexity, in its basic form it is a story of birth, death and eventual rebirth.

The various mysteries that surrounded this myth dramatized it in such a way that the initiate "became" one who died and rose again.

In effect, Demeter and Kore are one and the same. According to Jane Harrison, it was primarily in connection with agriculture that the Earth-goddess developed her double form.[53] Demeter is the civilized cultured earth, while Persephone is the young fruit of the earth. They represent the older and younger forms of the same person. Yet at the Eleusinian mysteries they each take on specialized forms. "Demeter," asserts Harrison, "becomes more and more agricultural, more and more the actual corn. The Mother takes the physical side while the Daughter that of the Underworld."[54] Demeter takes on the things of this life, such as laws and marriage. She becomes more approachable, a human goddess who eventually is taken up to Olympus. As for Persephone, the young form of the mother, she becomes removed from the human realm and associates herself more and more with things below and beyond.[55] The archetype of the feminine is thus split into an old and young, light and dark polarity.

This same split has also occurred in Mary. In our times, the Church seems more conscious of and concerned with the light side of Mary; so, as in the case of Demeter, the light side has ascended the throne, but Mary's dark Persephone side is deemed insignificant. While the light side is governed by a Christian Trinity, the black side is left an enigma. In the end, Mary is accepted into the Godhead and raised up, but her identity seems limited by her predominantly patriarchal setting. Her dark side, like Persephone, remains in the underworld—suggesting that the young and potentially fruitful affirmative side of the psyche is related to the nether regions of the unconscious. It also means that this side is furthest from consciousness. The now infertile Demeter is safe to bring onto Olympus, and the same is true with Mary. She may represent wisdom is this capacity, for she has tasted all, yet in the end she has been fatally separated from the earth. The life-bearing, nurturing, taking side of life is left to Persephone or to the aspect embodied by the Black Madonna.

Demeter as corn-mother represents the earth, but in the limited sense of grain-mother.[56] At the same time, Demeter carries earlier associations of a more general non-agricultural nature. Among these is her title of *Kourotrophos* (Child-Rearer). As such, she is often seen carrying two children, one in each arm. According to Harrison,

> Pausanias, when examining the chest of Cypselos, saw a design on which was represented "a woman carrying a white boy sleeping on her right arm; on the other arm she has a black boy who is like the one who is asleep; they both have their feet twisted; the inscriptions show that the boys are Death (the black one) and Sleep (the white one), and that Night is the nurse of both."[57]

To think of Mary as *Kourotrophos* is natural, for she is responsible for her child. She conceived and thus bore all those mysteries in her heart. It is not enough to just speak of Mary, but of Mary who gave birth to the Savior. At the same time, Mary holds her black boy in her left arm. This Child too is like the child of Death described by Pausanias; its mother is the Queen of the Underworld. Perhaps the connection may be weak or only appear so, yet it does make one wonder why Mary holds her son in her left arm and why he too is black. Indeed, even here his great deed is possibly foreshadowed—his life would not be that of the common man, would be filled with betrayal and end in death. Yet he is sustained and held by a wisdom beyond the grasp of consciousness.

The mysteries of Demeter and Persephone are mysteries of the processes of death and renewal, in both the natural order and in the psyche. The rites took place secretly, in underground cave-like structures (*megara*), for instance at the Thesmophoria and Eleusinian Mysteries. To rely once more on Harrison's words, "Megara itself, meaning at first a cave-dwelling, lived on in the megaron of kings' palaces and the temples of Olympian gods."[58] The Madonna of Einsiedeln also has a megara-like structure, the black marble shrine in which she stands, a chamber in which many experience their own transformation. She holds the divine child, a figure also revealed at the climax of the Eleusinian Mysteries. During these mysteries a messenger announced with a loud voice: "The great goddess has borne a divine boy, Brimo has borne Brimos!"[59] This is paralleled by our own Christian message: "Unto us a child is born" (Isaiah 9:6). The psyche can draw a message from the cry, since the mysteries of Eleusis are performed today in varied forms, in the unconscious depths of the individual psyche.

There are few outer mysteries left to us moderns, but the same need for renewal and transformation is experienced by us all. The child to be born is our own renewed psyche—a psyche which has to enter its own underworld sanctuary of the unconscious, to be nursed by the night of our soul, to know an inner death and to be given the promise of higher spiritual life. The ultimate symbol for this at Eleusis was a simple ear of corn which was cut down and from whose seeds new life was promised. That ear of corn is ourselves—the great mystery which knows not only the light of day but also the dark night of waiting and suffering. The Black Madonna lends herself to such a transformation and affirmation of the total person.

The Shulamite and Venus

In the Song of Songs, 1:5-6, we find:

> I am black but lovely, daughters of Jerusalem,
> like the tents of Kedar,
> . like the pavilions of Salmah.
> Take no notice of my swarthiness,
> it is the sun that has burnt me.[60]

The Shulamite woman is the bride in the Song of Songs who serenades and pursues her groom. They are united, separated, and finally reunited. The word Shulamite means "princess," as in chapter 6:13:

> Return, return, O Shulamite, return, return
> that we may look upon you.
> Why should you look upon the Shulamite,
> as upon a dance before two armies?[61]

Many have interpreted and used this Song in a variety of ways. The Talmudic scholars saw it allegorically as a relationship between God and Israel. The Christian Church saw it as one between Christ and his Church. Others saw it as simply a collection of hymns to love.[62] Many alchemical writings pick up on this love dialogue, as described in Jung's *Mysterium Coniunctionis*, where the Shulamite corresponds to the *nigredo*, the black initial stage of the alchemical process:

> The blackness of guilt has covered the bridal earth as with black paint. The Shulamite comes into the same category as those black goddesses (Isis, Artemis, Parvati, Mary) whose names mean "earth."[63]

She is that which must be transformed. In the end, there is to be a union of bride and groom, sun and moon, where the Shulamite will take on the attributes of the sun—that is, her head will be of gold.[64] The hair of the Virgin of Einsiedeln is also tinted with gold, as is the Child's. The unification of bride and groom is like that of unconscious and consciousness: each takes on attributes of the other, which is another way of saying that a reconciliation takes place between them. The Shulamite is earthy[65]; she is instinctual and primitive, the *prima materia*, the unconscious itself.[66] Her union with the groom, the sun, is both a redemption in the sense of keeping her from aimless wandering, and a renewal for the sun (consciousness) by directing his glance to that which is of the earth, and thus which is substantial and nourishing.

It may be true that the Shulamite represents on one side "the blackness of guilt," yet this guilt is experienced from a conscious viewpoint only. The Shulamite in herself is beautiful and lovely, as any superficial reading of the Song of Songs quickly shows:

"You are beautiful as Tirzah, my love, comely as Jerusalem, terrible as an army with banners. Turn your eyes from me, for they disturb me."[67] There is something appealing and enticing about the Shulamite woman, and it is in this sense that she has a Venus-like quality. She is simultaneously appealing and disturbing. The groom says:

> You ravish my heart, my sister, my promised bride,
> you ravish my heart with a single one of your
> glances, with one single pearl of your necklace.
> What spells lie in your love, my sister, my promised bride![68]

Here the Shulamite recalls what Venus originally was: a goddess of beauty and physical love. *Uenus* (Medieval Latin for Venus) is a personification of *uenus*, which is at once physical love, the art of love, the person loved, and such qualities as arouse love, especially charm, grace, and seductiveness.[69]

In context of the feminine principle, Venus plays a very important role. She is that quality that makes a woman attractive; it is her quality to attract earthly love. Hers is the appeal of the earth itself, in that the earth carries the feminine qualities of bringing forth, nourishing and taking back into itself. It has already been mentioned that the Black Virgin of Einsiedeln might bear some relationship to the Venus principle, particularly through the myth of Tannhäuser in the Venus Mountain. In addition, there definitely seems to be a Venus quality about the Black Virgin in terms of her attracting power in the lives of countless people. She has a quiet strength about her, though there are no great doctrines concerning her. She stands in her own shrine at the traditionally neglected end of the cathedral. She bears a look of modesty and passive wisdom, yet the entire monastic life and the life of Catholic Switzerland seems to center around her; in addition, thousands of non-Swiss and non-Catholic visitors crowd her shrine yearly. Her passive modesty is like a trick to the psyche, for behind her lies a power often foreign to consciousness. It is as though she outwardly represented those forces within all of us which impel us, in disturbing way, to look at life from a dimension and perspective hitherto unseen or unaccepted, and frequently diametrically opposed to known and cherished attitudes and ideas. This attracting quality has a purpose in that it seems to want to complete and compensate life. The unconscious calls whether we like it or not, and more often we do not. This is especially true when consciousness assumes too dogmatic and dominant a position, as is obviously the case in our overly rational, scientific Western culture. The more the irrational and illogical sides of life are denied, the more Venus-like and compensatory will they become.

It may not be amiss to suggest that the Black Virgin of Einsiedeln is enticing to so many simply because of her ability to draw the agony of death, senseless pain and suffering, meaninglessness, futility and a sense of loss out of a person's soul and into harsh but clear consciousness. In her case, there seems to be another quality in that she not only entices these out of a person; she also blesses them. She blesses our despair, so to speak. As a manifestation of the dark side of life and the psyche, she blesses these experiences as elements in the harmonious balance required if life is to have not only depth and continuity, but also hope and promise. She blesses the dark side of life and places the unanswerable in context of a greater master plan which lies, for the most part, outside consciousness. This master plan is often faithfully accepted within the context of a religious faith, or intuitively perceived, or seen *ex post facto* when one is near the end of one's life and can then see the design and plan which it has followed.

In the end, the Black Madonna speaks for herself, as will the collective norms. Like the Shulamite who seeks out her groom, the Black Virgin is mutually involved with her groom, collective consciousness, through a system of compensatory interactions whose ultimate aim is psychic-spiritual wholeness.

Chapter Four—Notes

[1]John Dawson, *A Classical Dictionary of Hindu Mythology*, p. 142

[2]*Ibid.*, p. 86

[3]*Man, Myth and Magic*, Vol. IV, p. 1556

[4]Heinrich Zimmer (a), *Philosophies of India*, p. 565

[5]*Ibid.*, p. 568

[6]C.G. Jung, *CW* IX, i, p. 82

[7]*Ibid.*

[8]*Ibid.*, p. 215

[9]Zimmer (b), *Myths and Symbols in Indian Art and Civilization*, p. 214

[10]*Ibid.*, p. 215

[11]Erich Neumann, *The Great Mother*, p. 278

[12]Zimmer (a), p. 566

[13]Zimmer (b), p. 211

[14]*Man, Myth and Magic*, Vol. IV, p. 1556

[15]Zimmer (b), p. 215

[16]It has been suggested that she and the child were mistaken by the early Christian community as the Virgin and Child, and that some of the Black Madonnas in Europe may have their origin in this fact. See Esther Harding, *Woman's Mysteries*, p. 185

[17]von Franz, *Apuleius' Golden Ass*, Chapter X, pp. 5-6

[18]*Ibid.*, material drawn from Chapter XI

[19]*Ibid.*, p. 2

[20]*Ibid.*, p. 3

[21]This issue is discussed in Chapter XI, pp. 14-18, in von Franz, *Apuleius' Golden Ass*

[22]*Ibid.*, Chapter X, p. 9

[23]Laurens van der Post, *Heart of the Hunter*, p. 195

[24]Harding, p. 184

[25]R.E. Witt, *Isis in the Graeco-Roman World*, p. 194

[26]Harding, p. 185

[27]*Ibid.*, p. 180

[28]*Ibid.*, p. 188

[29]Witt, p. 185

[30]*Ibid.*, pp. 193-194

[31]Harding, p. 188

[32]*Ibid.*

[33]Witt, p. 97

[34]Harding, p. 20

[35]*Ibid.*, pp. 20, 31

[36]C.G. Jung, *CW* V, pp. 317-318

[37]Harding, p. 31

[38]*Ibid.*, p. 25

[39]*The Random House Dictionary* (1967)

[40]Harding, p. 113

[41]*Ibid.*, p. 114

[42]*Ibid.*

[43]*Ibid.*

[44]*Ibid.*, pp. 111-112

[45]*Ibid.*, p. 100

[46]*Revised Standard Version*, verses 1-6

[47]Dorothy Luckie, "A Short Study of the Black Virgin," Vol. 3, #5

[48]Harding, p. 151

[49]*Ibid.*

[50]Sylvia Perera, *Descent to the Goddess*, p. 76

[51]Harding, p. 151

[52]*Ibid.*, p. 212

[53]Jane Harrison, *Prolegomena to the Study of Greek Religion*, p. 272

[54]*Ibid.*, p. 275

[55]*Ibid.*, p. 276

[56]*Ibid.*, p. 271

[57]*Ibid.*, p. 268

[58]*Ibid.*, p. 126

[59]C.G. Jung, *CW V*, p. 343

[60]Drawn from the *Jerusalem Bible*

[61]Drawn from the *Revised Standard Version*

[62]*Jerusalem Bible*, p. 991

[63]C.G. Jung, *CW XIV*, p. 420

[64]*Ibid.*, pp. 433-434

[65]*Ibid.*, p. 416

[66]*Ibid.*, p. 411

[67]*Revised Standard Version*, 6: 4-5

[68]*Jerusalem Bible*, 4: 9-10

[69]*Origins—A Short Etymological Dictionary of Modern English*, p. 764

5

THE DARK MOTHER AS IMAGE
OF EARTH AND PSYCHIC WHOLENESS

Teilhard de Chardin's confrontation with Matter is a concise and poetic echo of Meinrad's encounter with the Finsterwald:

The man fell prostrate to the ground
A great silence fell around him.
...a confused feeling that the force which had
swept down upon him was equivocal, turbid, the
combined essence of all evil and all goodness.
The hurricane was within himself.
And now...the tempest of life, infinitely gentle,
infinitely brutal was murmuring:

"You called me: here I am. Driven by the Spirit far from humanity's caravan routes, you dared to venture into the untouched wilderness; grown weary of abstractions, of attenuations, of the wordiness of social life, you wanted to pit yourself against Reality entire and untamed.

"You had need of me in order to grow; and I am waiting for you in order to be made holy.

"And now I am established on you for life, or for death. You can never go back, never return to commonplace gratifications or untroubled worship. He who has once seen me can

107

never forget me: he must either damn himself with me or save me with himself.

"I am the fire that consumes and the water that overthrows; I am the love that initiates and the truth that passes away. All that compels acceptance and all that brings renewal; all that breaks apart and all that binds together; power, experiment, progress—matter: all this am I.

"Because in my violence I sometimes slay my lovers; because he who touches me never knows what power he is unleashing, wise men fear me and curse me. They speak of me with scorn, calling me beggar-woman or witch or harlot; but their words are at variance with life, and the pharisees who condemn me, waste away in the outlook to which they confine themselves; they die of inanition and their disciples desert them because I am the essence of all that is tangible, and men cannot do without me.

"You who have grasped that the world has, even more than individuals, a soul to be redeemed, lay your whole being wide open to my inspiration, and receive the spirit of the earth which is to be saved.

"Son of earth, steep yourself in the sea of matter, bathe in its fiery waters, for it is the source of your life and your youthfulness.

"You must have oil for your limbs, blood for your veins, water for your soul, the world of reality for your intellect.

"Never say, 'Matter is accursed, matter is evil;' for there has come one who said, 'You will drink poisonous draughts and they shall not harm you,' and again, 'Life shall spring forth out of death,' and then finally, the words which spell my definitive liberation, 'This is my body.'

"Son of man, bathe yourself in the ocean of matter; plunge into it where it is deepest and most violent; struggle in its currents and drink of its waters. For it cradled you long ago in your preconscious existence; and it is that ocean that will raise you up to God"'

Meinrad was in essence an adventurer into his own soul. The Finsterwald that stood without was metaphoric of the Finsterwald within. And just as Matter stood before him in the un-

differentiated form of the dark forest, so it also stood within himself
to be redeemed—"You had need of me in order to grow; and I was
waiting for you in order to be made holy."

St. Meinrad took the statue of the Virgin with him. What did
he hope to gain? What did he gain? I would conjecture that it
was the side of the feminine which was not so noticeable or ac-
ceptable to the patriarchal light-side of life from which he came
and from which he sought refuge. This collective patriarchal side
of life saw the feminine in its own terms. The Virgin Mother was
made a part of the patriarchal world according to its own guidelines: "They speak of me with scorn, calling me beggar-woman
or witch or harlot; but their words are at a variance with life. . ."
This gap had to be filled in St. Meinrad's life, as it does in the
lives of countless individuals today. Just as the Finsterwald beck-
oned Meinrad, so the unconscious of mankind collectively and
individually throughout the centuries beckons entry into its "untouched wilderness." Just as the Black Madonna is a product of
refinement centuries in the making, so the psyche seeks its own
refinement from its crude undifferentiated beginnings: "Son of
man, bathe yourself in the ocean of matter. . .for it cradled you
long ago in your preconscious existence; and it is that ocean that
will raise you up to God."

It is not historic accident that popular demand had the Virgin
remain black following her renovation in 1799. These were common people, peasants who reacted from what can simply be called
a common or earth-oriented side of the soul. This common or
natural side in every person has a wisdom beyond that handed
down by traditional culture. Through their demand, they com-
pensated for the *status quo,* and they met their need for psychological balance. The attraction of the Black Madonna was felt
unconsciously, and it is to that side of the psyche that she makes
her greatest appeal.

This unconscious often acts as a maternal provider of wisdom
and insights, in addition to initiating the very process of healing
within the psyche. Though this healing aspect has already been

mentioned, it is very beautifully represented in the active imagination of a twenty-eight year old woman who suffered from an
inferiority complex. This inferiority was strongly related to her
very weak sense of her own femininity and the feeble instinctual
side that then went with it. Her central problem was essentially
the development of her femininity—in this case, an earthy femininity that could bring her into contact with the very natural
processes of life both within and without herself. All along she
felt she would never be a good partner for a man. In her own
words she writes:

> In my active imagination a *dark exotic madonna-like woman appeared*
> (which was not a figure from a dream but a form in which two
> real women join into one, a person I had met on my Sahara trip
> during Easter 1973).

> I would like to briefly describe these two meetings. With several
> other participants of the travel group, I roamed through one of
> the oases to that place. One of the Tuareg women, *in a black, long
> garment, a black cloth over her head,* drew near us and offered to
> sell us a piece of jewelry attached to a leather band—a quadratic
> metal plate (7x7cm) on which was engraved a beautiful design,
> *stressing the four corners and the center.* I looked at the piece and
> it pleased me very much. I asked about the price, which seemed
> to me, however, much too high and, as the woman did not bar-
> gain, we went further. After we had gone about 500 meters, it
> became suddenly clear to me that I absolutely wanted to own this
> piece of jewelry and ran quickly back. I found the woman in her
> hut, her child at her breast. When she saw me, she laughed, placed
> the child aside, got the piece from a sack and sold it to me.

> The meaning of this experience became known to me only some
> time after my return from the trip, when it struck me that it itself
> should be considered on the subjective level as a dream.

> *The dark woman in me,* my shadow, offers me a piece of jewelry
> which I do not accept at first, yet which I subsequently knew to
> be of great meaning for me. The impression and significance in
> it is that the piece of jewelry which my shadow presented to is
> *a mandala, a symbol for the Self.*

> The other experience goes as follows: on the same trip, I met also

another dark madonna-like woman, whose beauty and softness deeply impressed me, and so I photographed her.

A year after this trip, I tried an active imagination for the first time. To my astonishment, that woman whom I photographed appeared alive before my eyes. She wore the *usual long black garment,* in addition to a black cape which she had placed over her head and held together with both hands in front of her breasts, so that only her face and hands were visible. The features of her face were finely cut. The skin was a light brown and her eyes were cast down. About her soft mouth lay a slight smile. The hands were very long and narrow of a somewhat dark brown, like her face, while the fingernails were lacquered bright red.

As she stood there, with the garment itself moving lightly in the wind, fully peaceful, with an inward directed look, the slight smile, the hands gathered together over her breast, she emanated a great deal of softness, inner peace, patience, calmness and devotion. She reminded me of a madonna.

At the same time she emanated something so promisingly sensual, her beauty worked in a lively and earthy manner upon me that besides the impression to think I had a madonna before me, the impression appeared to have met one who is a gentle, devoted, tender, passionate lover.

Painfully, so that the tears mounted up for me in my eyes, my problem became clear or spoke out to me at the sight of this woman who revolved around it. I feared then I could miss my development to become a woman myself.

I began to speak to her somewhat as follows: You are so self-evidently a woman, as a flower is a flower and a tree is a tree. I, on the contrary, have so many problems with my becoming a woman. Often the fear tormented me that my experience could come to a dead stop – could not complete itself. You appear to me as one who possesses in rich measure all the feminine qualities I lack. I wish so much that you could advise and help me on my way to become a woman. Tell me, what can I do in order to develop your softness, your devotion, and love in me?

I spoke to her repeatedly, but she remained silent. It seemed to me as if her smile deepened, but she did not answer me.

After some time I tried to formulate an answer for myself which could have originated from her: "You should try to become more

sensual. I mean that you should use your senses quite differently
from before. You should train and sharpen all sense impressions
and experience them intensively. Likewise, it is important to admit in all intensity your feelings, even those which upset or ache
you."

Thus ends the attempt of my first active imagination. In June of
1974, I had a dream which I would bring in connection with the
active imagination: I had two different hands, my right was my
own, my left a brownish, very narrow fine hand whose touch was
especially soft and gentle.[2]

For the most part this account speaks for itself. It is interesting
to point out, however, the role that this dark-skinned, black-robed
madonna played for this woman psychically. She became the vehicle for filling in the gap of what was missing in her own nature,
namely, an earthy femininity related to life in a beautifully natural and instinctual way. This is very much related to the woman's
need for the quadratic engraved piece of jewelry which stressed
the four corners and the center. It was truly a symbol of her own
personality and her need for wholeness. The dark-skinned woman not only offered her the piece of jewelry, but herself became
the means to that earthy wholeness. She personified this specific
aspect of the woman's unconscious life which, once made conscious, acted as a healing force in her life by bringing about a
more reasonable psychic balance between the light and dark sides
of her femininity. For this woman, the closing dream shows she
was able to integrate this dark feminine power. Her right hand
is much more representative of her conscious personality. Her left
hand, however, is much more of her unconscious, and accordingly it acts to balance the right hand, showing that she has as-
similated the features of the dark-skinned madonna she described.
In the same manner, the Black Madonna of Einsiedeln does not
simply compensate a lack of femininity in our culture, but the
lack of a specific kind of femininity—a femininity that is dark and
acts as the matrix of all creativity and renewal.

The unconscious seems to seek consciousness of its own voli-
tion. This striving toward consciousness is such a powerful force

in both individual and collective history that at times one could wish that it had never started, since it entails an awareness of death and decay. The urge toward consciousness can pull a person in many directions, and at times destroy the individual if his ego is not strong enough, or if there is not a loving, supportive community or active and responsible rituals to carry him (or her) through the storms. It is as though the unconscious at times becomes violent in its efforts to become conscious, and at other times only appears violent because our world view becomes inverted by it.

Aside from this destructive side, the dark feminine is the missing fourth in the psychic diagram of wholeness. Jung himself suggested that the missing fourth in the Trinitarian principle is the feminine. The tremendous importance of the masculine-feminine polarity raises the question of how it is manifested in contemporary religious life, specifically the Judeo-Christianity of the Western world. The Black Madonna must be seen in this context in order for her present role to be more fully understood.

It takes little imagination to see that the feminine, generally speaking, has been relegated to a functionally inferior position in our patriarchal culture. Yet the feminine is always there and must express itself. It is not beyond reason that part of the explanation why the madonna is black is precisely this demeaned position; by her blackness, she seems to compensate the cultural one-sidedness which places more value on intellect and reason and conscious conquests than it does the deep mysterious processes of the soul. Her blackness boldly accentuates this defect, and by so doing, seems to stimulate individuals to a consciousness of her rightful place.

The lack of the feminine cannot without injury be tolerated either in the individual psyche or in organized religion. In both, the feminine element needs to be developed. Our culture's over-reliance on the big, the powerful, the dominant, on excess, forces a dangerous compensation. The extreme form of the one-sided yang (masculine) consciousness constellates an opposite yin (femi-

nine) response of equal intensity. The benignity of the Black
Madonna psychologically changes into a raging Kali of India. In
other words, the dark feminine energy of any person or culture,
with all its potential for healing, creativity, and renewal, can
through neglect become the same energy that sickens, uproots,
and destroys the best intents of individuals and nations. Humanity
in the end pays for this neglect.

The attitude of our times far too often reflects the words which
Ulrich Zwingli preached in 1516 at Einsiedeln at the Feast of All
Angels:

> Alas the Blood which streamed with love
>   from his dear pierced side,
> Is turned to gall and bitterness through avarice and pride.
> Thus doth the monk who puts his Lord to grief and open shame,
> This house a treasury of grace to all the world proclaim;
> And all the world the wily Priest beguiles with fond deceit,
> And setteth up the Virgin's shrine as God's own mercy-seat.
> Oh, let not such fond vanities your ransomed souls enthrall!
> A feast of lies, no angels' feast, is this high festival.'

To equate the Virgin's shrine with "God's own mercy seat" is theologically debatable, but certainly psychologically valid. Both the
Virgin and the unconscious can be seen as mediators between
the individual and the Logos-Father God. Theologically, the Virgin
becomes the means for the sinner to approach God more easily.
She mediates for him. Psychologically, the life principle interferes
with the Logos-conscious principle. What consciousness cannot
accept, the unconscious can. The unconscious depths and the
life principle are not always very concerned about right or wrong,
conventionally defined.

If we can speak of the dark side of the Godhead, then the dark
side of the Father becomes His judgments. This in effect is what
consciousness generally tries to do. The dark side of the mother,
however, is illogical, irrational, unwarranted and seemingly without meaning. This is the side that is hard to integrate. Why are
there hurricanes, earthquakes, natural catastrophes, unexpected

deaths, and diseases that eat away a person's body and soul for
no apparent reason? We could call it fate, but the term is unsatis-
fying; rather, it is the side of the Godhead that is irrational and
beyond our understanding, and that consciousness cannot
tolerate—yet it is the price that must be paid, the "other reality"
that is necessary if one is to live life, if it is to be played out fully.
To the Hindu, life is a play. I take this to mean that a person must
come to see beyond or through incongruities, but at the same
time be a part of them and recognize that life has no drama without them.

Drama is the backbone of individuation. Tragedy is the dark
side of purpose, for even in tragedy there is a truth standing above
our ordered world. Standing before the Virgin or the unconscious,
we do not ask cause and effect questions. Such questions are
addressed to the Logos-conscious discriminating side of life; but
before *her*, there is not even a logical answer at times. To tragedy
there *is* no answer; the question must not be asked of her, for
it is wasted and misdirected energy. What is needed are not explanations to satisfy the logical mind, but courage to face the situation and to redeem a meaning that could act as a transformative
principle in life.

Psychic wholeness becomes a possibility through the symbolism
of the Black Madonna, thus preventing psychic splits that can
lead to neuroses or psychoses. In the same way, through her, a
person does not let his or her libido (energy) go off in projection
on other people—a projection that would take on dark characteristics, such as racial prejudice, witch hunting, and class oppres-
sion. Whenever people or individuals do not accept their own
dark side, it is projected onto the nearest, most convenient object or personality. In addition, the dark side never has a chance
to find a rightful place in the individual and collective psyche.
Being excluded, the dark feminine will then often take on aggressive features. The Virgin Mary is one side of the life principle,
a light feminine side of the psyche; but the Black Madonna picks
up another side of this life principle, in relatively isolated places

such as Einsiedeln and Czestochowa in Poland. Here can be seen, in incarnated form, the black aspect of life and its right to exist. We need to become more aware of these black phenomena, yet not identify with them. In the end the Black Madonna is archetypal, that is, impersonal and greater than any one individual. The Black Madonna carries this side for the human psyche and thus makes the *psychic* Finsterwald more accessible. Without a Black Madonna figure, that is, without some kind of understanding and relationship to the dark feminine aspect of the psyche, there is no solution. One becomes a victim rather than a potential beneficiary of arbitrary psychic forces, and is stranded in one's search for meaning and value. The worst thing is that many people do not undertake the search, or even feel the need to.

The Black Madonna represents the unofficial acceptance of the fickle nature of life, doing just what she pleases but always with a wisdom that is beyond our reason and with a goal beyond our vision. She not only blesses the valley of tears but *is* the valley of tears. According to Erich Neumann,

> Thus modern man...discovers...that in the generating and nourishing, protective and transformative, feminine power of the unconscious, a wisdom is at work that is infinitely superior to the wisdom of man's waking consciousness, and that, as source of vision and symbol, of ritual and law, poetry and vision, intervenes, summoned or unsummoned, to save man and give direction to his life.[4]

This is a special wisdom of "loving participation"[5] with the psyche. The unconscious has a wisdom of its own, and though it seems at times to endanger the fragile ego, it also helps and redeems that same ego, often through the very dangers to which it is subjected.[6]

The Black Madonna of Einsiedeln is a compensatory psychic figure. She is an expression of the need for psychic-spiritual wholeness in an age and culture that has far over-valued the place of reason and the need for causal explanation. She is the result of this one-sidedness and serves to bridge the gap. Because of her

darkness, she is able to relate the dark side of the psyche to wholeness. The dark and rejected sides of the personality are given a
rightful place in the psychic structure. Just as the Black Virgin
was visited by prisoners and cripples and misfits and, in the case
of the Black Madonna of Chartres, prostitutes, so the unconscious
too knows a place for its rejected children of the conscious kingdom. What the collective order cannot accept, the Black Madonna
can. Similarly, what consciousness finds intolerable and unaccept-
able, the unconscious often readily accepts and, not rarely, uses
in more noble and valuable ways. This is felt quite keenly when
an individual becomes sick. It is as though another force had in-
truded itself and disrupted plans and weakened defenses. Sickness mercilessly twists the straight line of conscious programming.
Consciousness would go directly from A to E, but the unconscious would also include B, C, and D, and not necessarily in that
order. The conscious mind can anticipate the completed task or
the accomplished goal, but is at the mercy of the meandering influences of both external and internal forces. Sickness then can
be very important as a means to lead not only symbolically to
the reality of death, but also to a higher consciousness and a deeper
individuation.

For most individuals in the West, there is a need to tap into
the mystery of the Black Madonna and, through her, to taste,
in a compensatory manner, an aspect of life which is not only
important but essential for a full perspective on the rhythm with
which life moves. Not to know that rhythm—the process of birth,
life, and death—would doom anyone to naiveté and sentimentality, and to a world of undernourished piety and one-sided "wisdom." Whether speaking theologically of God or psychologically
of the Self, the issue of psycho-spiritual wholeness is identical.
In either case, the Black Madonna—or the archetype she
represents—is key.

One of the difficulties of talking about the Black Madonna of
Einsiedeln is the relative obscurity of this particular shrine. Com-
paratively few people have heard of this small community and

monastery, let alone of its Black Madonna. I have often wondered what and where her parallels might be in North America. I have certainly experienced her in my own interior world and have met her countless times in my analytic practice. The Dark Virgin is archetypal and her power thus exists in every person and every culture. The problem is that in many cultures the dark side of the feminine is incarnated in some venerated form which then assists the people in containing the energy surrounding her, helping them maintain a respectful attitude toward this power. This is not true in North America. There is no equivalent of Kali, Ereshkigal, Demeter in her black form, or the Shulamite, at least not in any external form. The dark feminine is expressed as an archetypal content from the collective unconscious and is intricately woven in the fabric of American history. Known or unknown, this dark feminine energy fulfills a dynamic role in the collective psyche of North Americans.

This collective dimension is impressively expressed in an active imagination (figure thirteen) experienced by the analysand Anna:

> Suddenly I see a megalopolis. It is Chicago. Underneath that giant city, deep inside the earth, I see a dark vault. Squeezed into that narrow dark vault is the Black Mother. She is bound, tortured, full of sores. Her tears run out of her eyes onto the earth and she cries out, "Behold and see, if there be any sorrow like unto my sorrow."

Perhaps at times it takes a person from another culture to see clearly what has happened to our own. The dark feminine does not live in the conscious collective psyche but rather below the megalopolis, "inside the earth...squeezed into [a] narrow dark vault...tortured, [and] full of sores"—in other words, deep in the unconscious. This short but impressive active imagination speaks well about what has happened to the dark feminine in our culture throughout its brief history. It has been forced to go underground. As with most unconscious contents, it will be felt either within the psyche or projected out onto some external person, thing or process. In our own culture the projection of the dark feminine is the dynamic behind out-and-out witch-hunts of many sorts. In subtler though more globally dangerous ways, the repression of the dark feminine was a factor behind such phenomena as black slavery, the near annihilation of the Native American, the degrading attitudes toward women and consequent heroic expectations of men, our attitudes towards our bodies, particularly our sexuality, and the way we treat the earth in general. In short, the black feminine symbolizes the earth and all that comes out of it or stands in relationship to it or, in one manner or another, represents it.

In my mind there have been three basic representatives of the earth in our predominately white culture. These three are women, blacks, and Native Americans. All three in one way or another have been projections of the earth with all of its instinctual, carnal, irrational and certainly frightening power. Because of this, all three have been degraded, looked down on, and forced to live out inferior roles and expectations. In some cases this has been obvious, in others quite subtle. This is all very complicated primarily because it is not just a matter of white attitudes doing this to women, blacks and Native Americans. Though recorded history may at times describe it as a distinct division between the good and the bad, such an analysis proves in the end to be far too naive and only serves to carry on more destructive projections. It is rather a matter of a style of consciousness which all parties have been actively involved in and affected by. It is a form of consciousness that has been decidedly masculine oriented on an archetypal level, with all of its rational, militaristic, conquest driven characteristics. It has put a wedge between spirit and matter, elevating the former. It has placed artificial divisions between men and women, black and white, Native American and European. It has forced us to look at the earth not as that which we are a part of and stand in relationship to, but as some *thing* to plow up, cut down, flatten, redirect, lay bare, extract from and, in short, to stand above and subdue. This sort of consciousness sees the earth not as endowed with the spirit of life, as a living organism, but as dead matter stripped of any potential sanctity.

It is as though our culture has all too easily sought to uproot itself from its own ground and, in its madness, make the earth its enemy. It is true that the earth can unleash frightening powers. Nature is unsentimental and unforgiving in its volcanic eruptions, droughts, floods and fires. There has been and always will be a primal struggle with all of nature for human survival. The earth can very quickly take back into itself what it has given. But the struggle with nature is different from its exploitation. Struggling to survive with nature can result in a harmonious cooperative relationship with it; while the result of our exploitation of the earth is epidemic despair (often mislabeled depression) and a sense of disconnectedness from our most elemental selves. In the language of the Taoist, our culture has been affected by a preponderance of the yang principle. This yang-masculine has become destructive simply because of its supremacy. The yin-feminine has been forced into exile, and consequently all have suffered. Men have been seduced to live out the life of the hero, forever seeking a dragon to kill, a maiden to rescue, a kingdom to claim. Women have been raised to applaud the drama, to deny their own heroic natures and simply not to question. Just how long these mythologems of the hero and damsel can last is tragically seen by the number of men and women who collapse under their weight at mid-life. The heroic struggles then hardly make sense and have little ability to carry the individuation process to deeper issues involving life's meaning and fulfillment. The feminine is denied as an integral part of a male's personality, leaving him all too frequently indifferent, insensitive, detached, unrelated and soul-sick.

With women things are a little different. The feminine yin is projected onto women in full force, but with two variations. On a conscious collective level, she is dressed according to societal standards. Here she carries the light side of the feminine yin, but almost always according to terms laid down by the yang consciousness which she herself also carries. To the extent that these terms are fulfilled, woman is honored and perhaps even venerated. By contrast, on the unconscious level the dark feminine yin is also projected onto woman. When this happens, she is often degraded and humiliated, seen as impertinent, a whore to be taken or a witch to be burned. Though men have certainly done this to women consciously and must assume just responsibility, on an unconscious level men and women together have participated in this yang consciousness and unwittingly conspired against the archetypal feminine in its darker aspects. It is not enough in our culture to say we must integrate the feminine, for this can all too easily turn into integrating what meets our conscious needs and wishes. We must especially talk about integrating the dark feminine, which is far more autonomous, life-oriented, and rooted in the earth.

The feminine, let alone the dark feminine, is not antithetical to the masculine archetype. To even imply this would be to perpetuate our culture's destructive divisions and imbalances of these archetypes. Left to itself, the feminine archetype would consolidate into a one-sided matriarchal mode of thinking with every bit of the destructive potential of an uncontrolled patriarchy. The present need for recognition of the feminine is only matched by its long-standing neglect. The task is to integrate what this dark feminine energy means instead of getting bogged down in just one more idealization of one more archetypal force.

Behind the repression of the dark feminine is the fear of the earth itself. The earth is symbolically the mother giving birth to all life and, in due time, takes everything back to herself. We are created from the dust of the earth and to dust we will again return. The earth reminds us of our own mortality, and as such is equated with an annihilator of consciousness. Any bid for consciousness demands an awareness of distinctions, the ego's separation of itself from what surrounds it. But when the ego denies its relatedness to its environment, these distinctions become separations which demand an unfair amount of power to maintain. The more power-driven the ego, the more the earth is feared and perceived as something to be conquered. Never before in history have we so sorely needed to reconnect ourselves with the earth, to find our place in the total ecological system, to reacquaint ourselves with Her mysteries, to revere Her giving and taking and to learn again that there is no spiritual life of any worth that is not rooted in the soil.

In this regard the following dream is highly interesting. The dreamer was a twenty-eight year old single white male who was experiencing a week-long spiritual retreat in a very primitive outdoor setting:

> I and a strange girl who is my partner are standing naked close to a flooded muddy creek, which is pouring over a small five-foot waterfall. We are standing fifty yards away from the flooded creek on the lower level of land. The five-foot drop in land extends on either side of the waterfall for quite a distance. The girl has dark hair to her shoulders and is my age. She expresses fear that the flood waters will sweep us along. I reassure her that the waters cannot reach us; however, at that moment, a wall of water rushes over the whole width of the five foot ledge, carrying us along with it. We swim with the current side by side. As we swim, I look up and see several hundred feet above us a huge rock overhang with the floodwaters threatening to pour over the edge and destroy us. The edge was directly overhead and the only way to survive was to keep swimming. The scene shifted and we were now standing on a sandbar created by the flood. The waters had abated and it was obvious that we were no longer in danger. Now a giant human hand, six or seven feet long, appeared. This hand fashioned a black figurine about eighteen inches high. The figurine looked like it was made of slate, had piled hair in a conical effect, an oriental face and a serene expression with a sort of half smile. She also had her arms crossed over her chest. Her feet were together.

The dreamer said that he felt what was taking place both within the dream and in waking life was of divine origin, pointing the way to a new life. It is certainly a dream of the earth and all the chthonic terror it can entail. The man was struggling for a deeper sense of his own identity, a search that would lead him beyond his own views and limited perspectives into the darkness of his own interior world. The world of Mother Nature became the backdrop for this drama, and it left him pondering Her mystery and strangeness. His more personalized relationship to the feminine within himself helped pave the way for the appearance of the darker, less familiar archetype. This is an initiatory dream which indeed provided the gift of a new image to meditate upon. It is a dream which intensified the symbol of death through drowning, but which led to renewal, thus assisting a decisive turning point in this man's life.

We are of the earth-mother and carry all the passions of life she has given to all creatures. We call these instincts, and have aimed a prejudicial glare toward them. We are afraid of our instincts and are, as Alan Watts says, "embarrassed to have a body." We are often inclined to apologize for the way our bodies function, for the demands they make, and for the shapes and postures they assume in the course of our own aging. No wonder that the body rebels and demands attention through a countless number of psychosomatic ailments.

Thus we are disembodied spirits forever seeking a home. We then depend too heavily on the rational realm of ideologies, be they political, scientific or religious. The more charismatic they become, the greater the danger of being dissociated from our true needs, leaving nations and individuals who are caught in this search withered and hollow for all their efforts. Any kind of spiritual aspiration undertaken hatefully against our own bodies or the body of the earth is doomed to end destructively.

The one group of people in our culture who have collectively maintained a spiritual relationship with the earth are Native Americans. Land and religion are the two great barriers that have separated the white and Indian communities in our history. The European saw land as something to possess, and spirituality as essentially unrelated to the soil. The Indian saw land not on the basis of ownership, but of relationship with spirituality intimately and intensely bonded to it. The earth was the Mother for the Indian, and there was no spiritual life disconnected from Her. The

differences in these two belief systems is the backbone of the tragic
history surrounding the relation of the two cultures. It was a collision of one fundamentally yang-masculine culture with another that allowed the yin-feminine side to manifest itself in the
darkness of the mysterious, life-giving earth.

One of the most impressive testimonies I have heard describ-
ing the Indian's view of spirituality and its relationship to the earth
was given by the Lakota Sioux holy man, Black Elk. In his description of the most sacred instrument of the Native American, the
pipe, he says:

> With this sacred pipe you will walk upon the Earth; for the Earth
> is your Grandmother and Mother, and She is sacred. Every step
> that is taken upon Her should be as a prayer. The bowl of this
> pipe is of red stone; it is the Earth...The stem of the pipe is of
> wood, and this represents all that grows upon the Earth...all the
> things of the universe are joined to you who smoke the pipe—all
> send their voices to *Waken-Tanka*, the Great Spirit. When you pray
> with this pipe, you pray for and with everything.[8]

To the "white" mind, the earth is dark and unknowable, dark both
in contrast to our collectively solar-oriented consciousness and
by virtue of her mystery. The words of Black Elk are echoed by
an active imagination (figure fourteen) experienced by Anna:

> I saw a big black woman who I knew to be a mother. She was
> gigantic. On top of her head, I saw two people making love, they
> were so comfortable in her hair, as if they were lying in a nest.
> The black woman had her hands crossed over her heart and her
> arms were filled with all kinds of warm-blooded animals that drank
> from her breasts. On her shoulders I saw all kinds of birds sitting
> and singing. On her body, around her navel, I saw all kinds of
> small animals like insects, cold-blooded animals, frogs, lizards,
> dragonflies, etc., which were happily enjoying their life and the
> closeness to her. Around the big black woman I saw, like a halo,
> living branches of plants, bushes and trees in bloom.

A month later she dreamed (figure fifteen):

> I woke up in the middle of the night and saw two big black hands
> in front of me. These were the hands of the Black Madonna. She
> was squatting or sitting on the earth and shaping all kinds of things
> out of the earth into lovely living shapes. She made birds and
> flowers that throbbed with life. She also created human beings
> out of the earth into warm living beings. Her hands were work-
> ing right in front of me. I saw them as if I was sitting in her lap,
> leaning against her heart. The hands were so big, as if I was a
> small child, seeing the hands of the mother. These hands were
> so dark and so very fine and sensitive and beautiful. I kept think-
> ing: She is the great Creator.

The inner world of this woman burst out in a number of similar
experiences, giving her an imagery of the earth with its teeming
drama of life, thus helping her gain a solid earth connection to
her spiritual development. Nine months later she dreamed:

> I threw myself with all my power onto the earth, or maybe I was
> pulled down by gravity somehow and surrendered. I fell on my
> knees in adoration. The earth was black and green grass grew out
> of it. And when I was on my knees and real close to the earth,
> I saw a clear crystal in front of me that was round and many-
> faceted. Inside of the crystal was a fiery red heart.

Only when she was close to the earth could she see the crystal
that contained the fiery red heart. The crystal is a symbol of wholeness and captures the unity of spirit and matter. This crystal is
filled with fiery passions which are revealed through, and held
together by, the many-faceted dimensions of wholeness. The earth
held this mystery for her within its dark life-giving abode; she
found a place for the dark feminine in her life. Her posture of
adoration is not one of terror and distance but of respect and
acceptance.

The Native American is more important to American culture
than most would believe. On a number of occasions Jung spoke
of the "Indianization" of most white Americans.' He based this
on the concept that the conqueror takes on the attributes of the
conquered. This is revealed in the number of states and cities that

carry Indian names, the increased interest in Indian culture and art, the popularity of Indian jewelry and clothing, and above all the appearance of Indian imagery in our dreams.

Raymond was a man in his early forties who consistently dreamed of Native Americans as a vital part of his own individuation process. He was married, white, the father of two children, and a responsible professional man. He was an ordained Protestant clergyman with an advanced degree in psychology. In time he became more and more aware that his spirituality and his psychological knowledge needed deeper connections with life itself and the land he lived on. He wanted to experience more deeply what Christian theology has long called the Incarnation, that is, the manifestation in matter of that which moves us spiritually. The following are just three of many "Indian" dreams that flowed quite spontaneously over the course of about four years:

> (1) I saw, as though I were a bird looking down on the earth, a town as it might have been a century ago. At the same time I saw an Indian on a horse who had fought a war in this town. I wondered what he wondered. He was on the edge of the community, and I wondered if he were now a statue or landmark. He seemed sad.

> (2) I had been attending a gathering of people on a farm. When it was over and I was leaving, I saw the contours of the farm land and realized or was told that those hills and contours were Indian mounds, and looking closer, saw they were burial mounds.

> (3) I brought my Indian ring to an Indian and told him it was very important I talk to him about it. I took it off and showed him how it needed to be rounded. He took it. I said it was silver and not imitation. As he started working on it, it broke. The ring was now much larger and more delicate than it had been. I immediately said it was okay and that I would get it fixed. But he said he would do it. Again I said he should not worry about it as I did not want to impose on him After I thought about it though, I decided to take him up on it.

From high up, this individual's (Raymond) spiritual overview could see the place of yesterday's collision of two cultures. He saw it as the stereotypic community on American soil. It was the routine mainstream of American life that had its roots of origin in the need to tame the wilderness and conquer its native dwellers. The Indian was the spiritual custodian of the earth, and it was he who stood in the way of western expansion which demanded land ownership by the common person, which in turn supported the notion of free enterprise. But it was all accomplished at a great price, for land and spirituality were deeply divided, as was the collective psyche. The concept of Incarnation as God in the earth was hardly considered. In the dream, the Indian is sad and is on the edge of the town, as only a landmark, perhaps. He was not included in the emergence of American consciousness. And today many look back at what others did to the Indian years ago, feel that collective guilt, and thus get caught in idealizing the Native American. The projections continue and will so long as any one fails to see, accept and understand the symbolic significance of the Indian within himself.

For Raymond, his unconscious was picking up the ancient ground of the land he knew as a member of the dominant culture. The very farmland, with its hills and contours, was in fact the burial place and religious site of its first dwellers. Raymond's psyche was deeply affected by the power of the land, and encouraging a more spiritual attitude toward it.

The understanding of earth-spirituality became more specific to him when he dreamed of taking his "Indian ring" to an Indian to make it rounder. The ring is a symbol of connection, relationship and wholeness. Raymond actually knew the Indian in his dream. The man he dreamed of was in waking reality an individual who had integrated Christian theology with his own traditional Native American spirituality. Raymond's own ring was no longer round and needed some work. When the ring broke, becoming larger and more delicate than it was before, Raymond took advantage of the willingness of his inner Indian shadow to repair and round out his consciousness.

Jung felt it critical that we understand that the Native American symbolizes the earth he stands on as well as the ancestral depths of his own soul, which is now affected by this soil. Most Americans are immigrants or the children of immigrants. Immigrants search for new ground and are affected by the spirit of the land upon which they make their new home. There is no way we can remain untouched by this ground and by those who dwelled upon it for nearly thirty thousand years. But the problem is that this "touching" is unconscious. Consciously, we are collectively separated from seeing the earth as our spiritual mother. For the most part we are still immigrants and children of immigrants in a strange land. The spirit of the land is forever there, beckoning in its own timeless way to the spiritual roots of all our endeavors. Earth darkness calls out to soul darkness and soul struggles to reply. Though there is nothing in this country akin to the Black Madonna of Einsiedeln to assist us, her archetypal energy is in the earth and within our own unconscious, awaiting its liberation. To turn our backs on her spells our own defeat; to search her out beneath the concrete and rubble of our culture and invite her return to our personal lives guarantees our renewal.

Chapter Five—Notes

[1]Teilhard de Chardin, selections from "The Spiritual Power of Matter," in *Hymn of the Universe*, pp. 60-65

[2]Translation and emphases mine. This active imagination was graciously shared with me by Dr. Adolf Ammann of Zürich

[3]From the sermon preached at Einsiedeln and entitled "Neither In This Mountain Nor Yet At Jerusalem," 1516, by Ulrich Zwingli. In Hatchards, *"Neither At This Mountain Nor Yet At Jerusalem": A Sermon Suited to the Present Time*, London 1869

[4]Erich Neumann, *The Great Mother*, p. 330

[5]*Ibid.*, p. 331

[6]*Ibid.*, p. 330

[7]Alan Watts, *Nature: Man and Woman*, p. 97

[8]*The Sacred Pipe*. Recorded and edited by Joseph Epes Brown, 1953

[9]Jung's discussion of the "Indianization" of Europeans in America can be found in the following sources (for the first three, see the *Collected Works*):
"Mind and Earth," 1927
"The Role of the Unconscious," 1918
"The Complications of the American Psyche," 1930
Memories, Dreams, Reflections, 1961

Bibliography

Amman, A.N. *Tannhäuser im Venusberg*. Zurich: Origo Verlag, 1964

Bennet, Anne R. *Einsiedeln "in the darkwood."* London: Burns and Oates, 1883

Brockhaus, F.A. *Der Grosse Brockhaus*. Vol. 7. Wiesbaden, 1955

Chardin, Pierre Teilhard de. *Hymn of the Universe. New York: Harper and Row, Publishers, 1965*

Cirlot, J.E. A Dictionary of Symbols. Translated from the Spanish by Jack Sage. New York: Philosophical Library, 1962

Corolla Heremitana. Hrsg. von A. Schmid. Neue Beitrge zur Kunst und Geschichte Einsiedelns und der Innerschweiz (Festgabe fr L. Birchler). Olten, 1964

Dawson, John. *A Classical Dictionary of Hindu Mythology.* London: Routledge and Kegan Paul, 1961

Dictionnaire des symboles. Paris: Editions Robert Laffont et Editions Jupiter, 1969

Fierz, H.K. "Psychological Discussion of the Tarot Marseille." Lecture at the Zurich C.G. Jung Institute during the winter semester 1972-1973, and again in the summer semester 1975

Franz, Marie-Louise von. *Shadow and Evil in Fairytales*. Zurich: Spring Publications, 1974

Harding, M. Esther. *Woman's Mysteries: Ancient and Modern.* Published by G.P. Putnam's Sons, New York, for the C.G. Jung Foundation for Analytical Psychology, 1971

Harrison, Jane Ellen. *Prolegomena to the Study of Greek Religion*. Third Edition. Cambridge, England: Cambridge University Press, 1922

Hastings, James, Ed. *Encyclopedia of Religion and Ethics*. Edinburgh and New York, 1908-1927.

Helbling, O.S.B., Dr. P. Leo. *Das Blockbuch von Sankt Meinrad und Seinen Mörden und vom Ursprung von Einsiedeln*. Einsiedeln: Benziger Verlag, 1961

Henggeler O.S.B., Dom. Rodolphe. *Brief Guide to the Abbey of Our Lady of the Hermits*. Translated by Susanne Felchlin-Eppes. Einsiedeln: Karl EberleBirchler Verlag (no date)

The Jerusalem Bible. General Editor, Alexander Jones. Garden City: Doubleday and Company, Inc., 1966

Jung, C.G. CW V, *Symbols of Transformation*. Princeton: Princeton University Press, 1967

Jung, C.G. CW IX, 1, *The Archetypes and the Collective Unconscious*. Princeton: Princeton University Press, 1968

Jung, C.G. CW IX, 2, *Aion*. Princeton: Princeton University Press, 1959

Jung, C.G. CW XI, *Psychology and Religion: East and West*. Princeton: Princeton University Press, 1969

Jung, C.G. CW XII, *Psychology and Alchemy*. Princeton: Princeton University Press, 1968

Jung, C.G. CW XIII, *Alchemical Studies*. Princeton: Princeton University Press, 1967

Jung, C.G. CW XIV, *Mysterium Coniunctionis*. Princeton: Princeton University Press, 1963

Jung, Emma, and Marie-Louise von Franz. *The Grail Legend*. Translated by Andrea Dykes. Boston: Sigo Press, 1986

Man, Myth and Magic. Richard Cavendish, Ed. London: Published by Purnell for BPC Publishing Ltd., 1970

Müller-Guggenbühl, Fritz. *Swiss-Alpine Folk Tales*. London: Oxford University Press, 1969

Neumann, Erich. *The Great Mother*. Bollingen Series XLVII. Princeton: Princeton University Press, 1970

Partridge, Eric. *Origins: A Short Etymological Dictionary of Modern English*. London: Routledge and Kegan Paul, 1963

Räber O.S.B., Dom. Ludwig. *Our Lady of Hermits*. Einsiedeln: Benziger and Co. Ltd., 1949

The Revised Standard Version of the Bible. Philadelphia: A.J. Holman Company, 1962

Ringholz, O. *Wallfahrtsgeschichte U.L. Frau von Einsiedeln*. Frieburg, 1896

Ulanov, Ann Belford. *The Feminine in Jungian Psychology and in Christian Theology*. Evanston: Northwestern University Press, 1971

van der Post, Laurens. *Heart of the Hunter*. London: Hogarth Press, 1961

Vita S. Meginrati. Ed. O. Holder-Egger in MG, SSXV. 445ss in Einsiedeln Library.

Wickram, Jrg (from Kolmar in Elsass). Records of the Town Clerk at Burgheim, recorded in the year 1555

Witt, R.E. *Isis in the Graeco-Roman World*. H.H. Scullard, General Editor. London: Thames and Hudson, 1971

Zimmer, Heinrich. *Myths and Symbols in Indian Art and Civilization*. Joseph Campbell, Ed. Bollingen Series VI. New York: Pantheon Books, 1946

Zimmer, Heinrich. *Philosophies of India*. Joseph Campbell, Ed. New York: Published by Pantheon Books for the Bollingen Foundation, Inc., 1951

Zingg, P. Thaddus. *Das Kleid der Einsiedler Muttergottes*. Einsiedeln: Ausliefer Benziger, Graphischer Betreib, 1974

Zwingli, Ulrich. "Neither in this Mountain nor yet at Jerusalem: A Sermon Suited to the Present Times." Preached at the Feast of All Angels, Einsiedeln, Switzerland, 1516. Printed in a booklet by Hatchards, 187 Picadilly, W. London, 1869

Index

SIGO PRESS

SIGO PRESS publishes books in psychology which continue the work of C.G. Jung, the great Swiss psychoanalyst and founder of analytical psychology. Each season SIGO brings out a small but distinctive list of titles intended to make a lasting contribution to psychology and human thought. These books are invaluable reading for Jungians, psychologists, students and scholars and provide enrichment and insight to general readers as well. In the Jungian Classics Series, well-known Jungian works are brought back into print in popular editions.

Other Titles from Sigo Press

Recovering from Incest *by Evangeline Kane*

Longing for Paradise *by Mario A. Jacoby*

Emotional Child Abuse *by Joel Covitz*

Dreams of a Woman *by Shelia Moon*

Androgyny *by June Singer*

The Dream-The Vision of the Night *by Max Zeller*

Sandplay Studies *by Bradway et al.*

Symbols Come Alive in the Sand *by Evelyn Dundas*

Inner World of Childhood *by Frances G. Wickes*

Inner World of Man *by Frances G. Wickes*

Inner World of Choice *by Frances G. Wickes*

Available from your local bookseller. If unavailable, you may contact SIGO PRESS, 25 New Chardon Street, #8748A, Boston, Massachusetts, 02114.